WALKING

OUTDOOR PURSUITS SERIES

Ruth Rudner

Human Kinetics

ging-in-Publication Data

Includes index.
ISBN 0-87322-668-2 (pbk.)
1. Walking--Handbooks, manuals, etc.   2. Hiking--Handbooks,
manuals, etc.   I. Title.   II. Series.
GV199.5.R83   1996
796.51--dc20

95-1520
CIP

ISBN: 0-87322-668-2

Copyright © 1996 by Human Kinetics Publishers, Inc.

Series Editor and Developmental Editor: Holly Gilly; **Assistant Editor:** Kirby Mittelmeier; **Copyeditor:** John Wentworth; **Proofreader:** Jim Burns; **Photo Editor:** Boyd LaFoon; **Index:** Joan Griffitts; **Typesetter:** Ruby Zimmerman; **Text Designer:** Keith Blomberg; **Layout Artist:** Stuart Cartwright; **Cover Designer:** Jack Davis; **Cover Photo:** © Larry Pierce/F-Stock; **Illustrator:** Thomas • Bradley Illustration & Design

Human Kinetics books are available at special discounts for bulk purchase. Special editions or book excerpts can also be created to specification. For details, contact the Special Sales Manager at Human Kinetics.

Printed in Hong Kong   10 9 8 7 6 5 4 3 2 1

Human Kinetics
P.O. Box 5076, Champaign, IL 61825-5076
1-800-747-4457

Canada: Human Kinetics, Box 24040, Windsor, ON N8Y 4Y9
1-800-465-7301 (in Canada only)

Europe: Human Kinetics, P.O. Box IW14, Leeds LS16 6TR, United Kingdom
(44) 1132 781708

Australia: Human Kinetics, 2 Ingrid Street, Clapham 5062, South Australia
(08) 371 3755

New Zealand: Human Kinetics, P.O. Box 105-231, Auckland 1
(09) 523 3462

CONTENTS

1

GOING WALKING

One bright autumn Sunday afternoon, I left the village of Igls, a couple of miles from and a thousand feet above Innsbruck in the Austrian Tyrol, to go for a walk. The air was crisp, the world shimmering with the gold of larch trees and birches. The pretty forest path was well-trod by about 200 years of walkers. I was headed for a mountain hut a few miles distant for an afternoon coffee and cake. On the way, I came upon an old woman walking up the path, holding the hand of a tiny girl. The girl was little enough that walking must have been a new activity for her. The two kept pace with one another, their footsteps matching. It struck me, in that moment, that I was seeing the ending and the beginning of life; that the rhythm of age and childhood were in accord; and that all of this was happening on foot.

Walking, indeed, spans a life. For all the years of our lives, it provides us the same thing it offers in the very beginning—the possibility of adventure and exploration. Walking is the ultimate act of independence, the activity that allows us to operate on our own whether we are 2 or 92.

If you are ready to leave father and mother, brother and sister, and wife and child and friends, and never see them again—if you have paid your debts, and made your will, and settled all your affairs, and are a free man, then you are ready for a walk.

—Henry David Thoreau

Walking is an activity that can span a lifetime.

I was about 2 years old when I went for my first *real* walk. My father took me into the woods at the end of our street, where we walked along a gentle path, then up what seemed to me a high hill. I remember my pride at reaching the top. I felt *very* big. When, on top, we sat down to rest, my father took a chocolate bar from his pocket and split it in half. My half was as big as his. I understood in that moment that we were equals.

Equal is what walking makes of us all. Although competitive walking exists, going for a walk is not competitive. You needn't be an athlete or skilled outdoorsperson, undergo training or purchase special equipment, or go to a particular place to go for a walk. Walking is different from any other activity on earth that is good for you in that nothing at all is required, except the good fortune to have legs that work.

For most of us, few things are more natural than walking. We do not think of it as a technical event requiring the synchronization of many of the body's more than 200 bones, over 650 muscles, and some 70,000 miles (112,000 km) of circulatory channels. To walk, we just walk.

So when you put on your old clothes and take to the road, you make at least a right gesture. You get into your right place in the world in the right way. Even if your tramping expedition is a mere jest, a jaunt, a spree, you are apt to feel the benefits of getting into a right relation toward God, Nature, and your fellow man. You get into an air that is refreshing and free. You liberate yourself from the tacit assumption of your everyday life.

—Stephen Graham

What Type of Walking Interests You?

There are any number of ways to go for a walk. You can amble along your way, or speed it up and walk for exercise. You can walk for pleasure, to sightsee, to rid yourself of tensions, to find solitude, to get from one place to another, to think out a problem, to daydream—or to get fit in the easiest possible way. You can enter into competitive walking (racewalking), fitness walking, distance walking, or orienteering. You can become a hiker or backpacker.

Walks around a suburban block or down a city street often lead to walks in the woods or mountains or other wild places. A joy for walking might entice you to join walking clubs or get involved in orienteering, which is nothing more than walking from point to point with the aid of a map and compass. There have been some interesting experiments lately with night walking, which leads to a whole new awareness of how your senses operate. Two New Mexicans, psychotherapist and author Nelson Zink and publisher Stephen Parks, writing in the fall 1991 issue of *Whole Earth Review*, reported on the enhancement of all their senses—hearing, balance, touch, smell—upon spending time walking at night, exploring the dark with peripheral vision. "With the calm of nightwalking, we discovered that anxiety and fear of the dark, so common in our culture, are effectively eliminated. Fear, anxiety and even physical pain are seemingly associated with focused vision, while peripheral processes engender relaxation and delight. . . ."

As for differences between walking and hiking, there are none. Because for some people the word *hiking* implies a wilder setting or a more challenging path, it may sound psychologically easier to simply *go for a walk*. But, in fact, no matter what you call it, the activity is the same.

© F-Stock/Kevin Syms

The difference between a walk and a hike lies merely in the trappings.

Types of Walking

If you have been living a sedentary life but have now decided you'd like to do some walking, the thing you need to do is go for a walk. For the variety of ways to walk to unfold, you must simply get off the couch.

It is walking itself that is the only prerequisite to finding your own particular walking niche.

The easiest way to go for a walk is simply to go out your door and walk.

Or, rather, the easiest way of getting into the *habit* of walking is to do that. Habit, after all, is about having things as easy as possible. When you know the walk is just out your door, so that no effort is required to get to it, it may be easier to do it regularly. For many people, exercise of any sort is not the problem, but the effort of getting *to* the exercise or ready for the exercise allows them to put it off. If the idea of walking is not in itself alluring, make doing it as easy on yourself as possible. There is nothing wrong with this. No exercise is about suffering.

Once you become a confirmed walker, city or suburban streets may still offer both ease and pleasure for the walks you do daily. On the other hand,

FINDING YOUR WALKING NICHE

Once you've decided to walk, here are some questions you might want to ask yourself:

Is seeing other people on my walk a part of the pleasure? Do I want to interact with others as I walk? Am I nervous alone but comfortable with a group or a partner? Or do I prefer solitude? Do I want to be alone to think?

Do I feel most comfortable on city streets, country roads, or woodland paths?

Do I need scenery to make me happy on a walk, or is the movement of walking enough to satisfy me?

How much time can I give to my walk? How much time can I give to *getting* to my walk?

Do I need the edge of competition to keep me at any activity, or do I progress best without that pressure?

What do I want to get from walking?

Can I incorporate walking into my daily routine, such as walking to and from work, or do I need to set aside a special time?

when walking becomes a habit, you may look for nearby paths that offer the softness of earth rather than pavement to walk upon; the opportunity to look at a different scenery; and the chance to observe wildlife and the movement of nature through time—which, by the way, you can do as well in city parks as in deep country. Once you have eased into walking in nature, you may begin to look for opportunities to go farther afield. These opportunities abound in urban areas (sometimes with more ease of accessibility) as much as they do in the countryside.

Are You In or Out?

You can, of course, walk without ever stepping foot outdoors. Treadmills provide excellent exercise and are not a bad idea if the weather is too ghastly to go outdoors (provided you have access to one). Many dedicated walkers move into the protection of malls when the weather gets too hot or too cold, too snowy or too wet. Malls frequently open their doors early for walkers, and many sponsor clubs or walking programs with the cooperation of local hospitals or health bureaus. For information about such programs, call the mall office. If there is no official program, there is still nothing to stop you from walking in the mall. You are bound to find other people doing the same.

There are other places—zoos and aquariums, for instance—that also open their doors early for indoor walkers. Information about these is usually available from local walking clubs. Superb places for indoor walking are large airports, where waiting for a delayed plane may be much more pleasant if you go for a walk.

Although indoor walking is sometimes advantageous, the concern of this book is with walking outdoors. Walking outdoors includes just about anything. Walking the dog. Walking to work. Walking to the corner store for a carton of milk. Walking vigorously along city sidewalks or through a city park or around a running track. Walking down a country road or on a woodland path or along the seashore. Walking in mountains and forests. Walking the miles of railroad beds or canal towpaths converted to walking trails across America. For that matter, walking across America.

You can walk for 20 minutes or an hour or a day. You can walk day after day after day. It is all the same activity, just suited to fit your own way of life and your need to feel your body move through space in the way for which it was created.

Getting Started

Not much is required to start walking. Of prime importance is the will to get up and walk. You'll also need a comfortable pair of shoes and a short amount

© F-Stock/Kristen Olenick

Walking is personal and allows you to enter into your surroundings in the fullest possible way.

of time. *Any* time spent walking is better than no time. Start gently. There's no need to push. If you've been sedentary, take whatever time you need to build up endurance. Don't push yourself away from the pleasure of walking, or the pleasure of a good habit you can enjoy forever. Among all the possibilities for getting and staying in good physical condition, walking is the easiest on our bodies and, therefore, the activity most likely to last a lifetime. It will, at the same time, make that lifetime feel better.

Walking is the only exercise in which the rate of participation does not decline in the middle and later years. In fact, in one national survey reported by The President's Council on Physical Fitness and Sports, the highest percentage of regular walkers for any group (39.4%) was found among men 65 years of age and older.

Walking is personal. It doesn't matter what anybody else says about time and distance, your own time and distance are your only concern.

Walking Clubs

For some people, exercise is easier if somebody else organizes it. Being with other people who are doing the same thing also helps. Even if, somewhere down the road, you opt to walk alone, joining a walking club can make starting easier. A club will provide you with information about shoes and other gear and give you access to good local walks. Clubs often sponsor local walking events you might find enjoyable. If the club is connected with any of the larger walking clubs—such as the Walking Club Alliance or the Prevention Walking Club—it can also provide you with information about national or international walking events. For information about walking clubs outside of the United States, check with your local outdoor shops. In Australia some clubs are listed in the telephone directory under *Clubs—bushwalking*. In Europe, the national alpine clubs are associations for walkers as much as for climbers and can give you information about trails and occasional *Volksmarsches*, although they do not offer regular gatherings just to go for a walk.

If a club interests you, your town's parks and recreation department will probably have information on those that exist in your area. Another source

© Parks Canada—Lynch

Walking clubs are a great way to find out about and experience good local walks.

of information is the Walking Club Alliance sponsored by *Walking Magazine*. About a thousand clubs in the United States and Canada—and a few on scattered United States military bases outside of the United States—are part of the alliance. The clubs run a huge gamut, from the informal gathering of five people who get together at lunchtime for a walk, to highly organized associations with hundreds of members. And they include everything—community clubs, corporate clubs, mall walkers, hikers, racewalkers, mothers pushing baby strollers, and recreational walkers of all sorts. The alliance can tell you if there is a club in your area, or help you start a club if there is none. Drop them a note at Walking Club Alliance, Walking Inc., 9-11 Harcourt Street, Boston, Massachusetts 02116. Tell them what your special interest is—recreational walking, racewalking, hiking, and so on—as there may be several different clubs in your area.

Walking Magazine publishes an events calendar in every issue. Competitive, charitable, and fun walking events, as well as racewalking events, are listed by region. These events are open to anyone, and each listing carries a phone number for more information. (If your club wants to list walking events in this calendar, information must be sent to them 4 to 6 months in advance to meet their publishing schedule.)

If you don't require a club immediately at hand, *Prevention* magazine's walking club can still provide you a framework for your own walking. For a membership fee of under $10, you receive their *Walker's World Handbook* and their bimonthly *Walker's World Newsletter*. The club holds an annual walkers' convention (the All-American Walkers Rally), which consists of 3 days of seminars led by walking, health, and nutrition experts; a chance to look at walking-related products; and a lot of walks. For more information, write to *Prevention* Walking Club, 33 East Minor Street, Emmaus, Pennsylvania 18098.

Traveling

Many cities have drawn up specific walking tours of their historic districts and other areas of special interest. Route maps are usually available from the city's chamber of commerce (or the tourist office in European, Australian, or New Zealand cities) or in guidebooks available in city bookstores.

Commercial outfits specialize in walking tours of all levels. They may tour cities, ancient ruins, parks, or Himalayan peaks. They may take you from inn to inn through lovely countryside or from hut to hut in the Alps. While some of these walking tours are easy and others challenging, all require a certain level of fitness. Even if they didn't, you wouldn't have any fun if you were suffering (nor would anyone else if you were complaining).

There is no better way to get to know any place on earth then to walk through it. You *feel* the place in a way you cannot when you are transported in a vehicle. You cover fewer miles when you walk than when you ride, but you gain so much more in experience that you end up having been more fully in the place than if you had ridden through 10 times as much of it. You *learn* something when you walk, whereas you merely pass through when you ride.

© Photo Network/Phyllis Picardi

Walking allows you to learn something new about a place, even if it's a neighborhood walk you've done countless times.

On Your Way

And, whether it matters to you or not, by becoming a walker you join an elite group. Many "tourists" wonder why anyone would deliberately choose to walk when there are so many other ways to get around. Once, when a friend and I were walking up a mountain path, we came upon a group of men on horseback going down. Each man had a fishing rod tied to his saddle. The men stopped to pass the time of day.

"Going fishing?" they asked.

"No," we said. "We're just backpacking."

"You mean you *walked* all this way and you're not even going fishing . . . ?!"

It's not infrequent that nonwalkers wonder why anybody would walk if they have a choice. To cross a mountain on foot requires time and energy you would not have to expend if you rode a horse over it, drove a car through it in some marvel of a tunnel blasted and carved out of solid rock, or flew over it in an airplane offering vast and spectacular views of half the world at once. Why, then, walk?

Is it reason enough to think that perhaps the mountain (or the forest or the meadow or the valley or the city) matters more than time? More than what lies beyond it? Is it reason enough to find yourself not contained in a machine, packaged, held prisoner, coddled and lulled to passivity at excessively high speeds? Is it reason enough to believe that, in life, it is the *road* that matters, not the end? I, for one, am in no rush to reach the end.

Anywhere you walk instead of ride, you are on your way. Getting started walking really means simply taking notice of what you have always done. Even a fisherman on horseback has to walk out to get his horse.

We are under-exercised as a nation. We look instead of play. We ride instead of walk.

—John F. Kennedy,
addressing the
National Football Foundation, 1961

2

WALKING APPAREL

Walking is *not* an expensive
sport. The only thing you really need is a pair of good, sturdy, comfortable
shoes. You could walk nude if it weren't illegal—and if you didn't pass too
close to brambles. Some people choose to walk without shoes. In addition
to various aboriginal peoples, there are those like the great Austrian
mountaineer Hermann Buhl, who trained by climbing the mountains around
his native Innsbruck in his stocking feet. You do not need to do this.

> *Few [people] know how to take a walk. The qualifications . . . are
> endurance, plain clothes, old shoes, an eye for Nature, good humor,
> vast curiosity, good speech, good silence and nothing too much.*
> —Ralph Waldo Emerson

You do not need to buy special clothes for walking, although modern
fabrics have been engineered to provide maximum weather protection
without bulk and with minimal weight, so, if you want to buy something,
you'd do well to look at these new fabrics. Appropriate clothes for weather
and seasons allow you to walk year-round comfortably, regardless of

weather. If you're walking for exercise, you do not want to be stopped by rain, snow, or cold.

Getting Dressed

What constitutes appropriate clothes? In any season besides summer, when shorts, loose trousers, or skirts that allow for an easy stride all work nicely, layering is the way to go. If you are walking briskly, it won't take long to get warm, even on a cool day. Make sure you are wearing things you can take off and wrap around your waist or, better yet, throw into a small rucksack you carry on your back. You want outerwear that will protect you from the elements so that you can walk in rain, snow, or wind and still feel comfortable. You want underwear that does not hold moisture against your skin to chill you.

© F-Stock/Caroline Wood

Wearing appropriate clothing will heighten the enjoyment of your walks.

There is a real technology to dressing for sports and, while you can manage to go for a stroll without it, if you begin fitness walking, race-walking, or serious hiking, it is a technology you may find handy.

Your first layer should be polypropylene underwear. (Helly Hanson Prolite 5000 is considered best by Greg Caracciolo at Bozeman, Montana's Northern Lights outdoors shop. I've been asking Greg to tell me what I need and why I need it for the past 10 years and have yet to make a mistake with a purchase.) Polypro is the fiber that absorbs the least amount of moisture from your skin. Perspiration simply passes through this layer, leaving your skin dry. (Your body loses heat 35 times faster when wet. In cold weather, you cannot afford this loss.)

The second layer can be any of the polyester fleeces, or heavyweight or midweight underwear, such as Patagonia's Capilene. This is your insulating layer, absorbing the moisture that passes through the polypropylene layer.

The third layer is a shell made of any of the microfiber nylons and polyesters or, the newest stuff, the 100% windproof, highly breathable Gore products. (This is the company that developed Gore-Tex, the first water-proof yet breathable fabric on the market. Gore basically revolutionized outdoor clothing, making it possible to keep dry from rain, yet not soaked by your own sweat that could not evaporate through earlier waterproof fabrics.) For this layer, you need something windproof, and if you're walking in a wet climate, you want something as waterproof as possible as well. The best of these new products are Patagonia's Pneumatic Gear and Gore's Windstopper.

On the bottom, you want lightweight long underwear with a second layer of lycra tights. Again, a stroller can be comfortable in anything, but the serious walker might like the extra support lycra tights give to muscles. Athletes wear tights because the extra support helps prevent injuries. (If you're walking fast and somehow slip in a way that could pull a hamstring, it would be less apt to happen if you were wearing tights.) In very cold weather you can add a pair of windpants or fleece pants on top of your tights.

None of this stuff is cheap, but all of it will last more or less forever, and it can all be used year-round for any number of sports—walking, running, skiing, biking, and more. My tights have proved wonderful for canoeing in cold weather.

Fleece hats and headbands (all of which are better than wool because they won't make your head itch) range from $10 to $30. Hats matter. You lose over 70% of your body's heat through your head. I was always told that if my feet were cold, I should put on my hat. (And I do.)

Fleece gloves with Windstopper inside range from $40 to $50. You can also buy polypropylene liners for your old gloves for about $7. There are polypropylene sock liners available, as well. These not only help keep your

APPROXIMATE COSTS OF HIGH-TECH WALKING CLOTHES*

Lightweight underwear	$20–$30, bottoms
	$20–$30, tops
Midweight Capilene	$30–$40, bottoms
	$35–$50, tops
Fleece insulating layers	$50–$90, bottoms
	$50–$110, tops

The big differences in these fleece garments have to do with weight, stretch, and style. The heavier the fabric, the more expensive the garment.

Shells	$60–$300
Pants	$50–$175

These prices reflect fabrics that range from basic nylon up to Gore-Tex.

Lycra tights	$40–$100

*Prices are given in U.S. dollars.

feet warmer but, as a thin undersock, give you added protection against blisters. In hot sun, a hat with a brim protects the top of your head, your face, and your neck from too much sun.

If you are going to outfit yourself with clothes for walking, go to a good outdoor shop or running shop, where you can find both high-quality garments and a staff knowledgeable about their stock. You need to be able to ask questions and get good answers. Often, quality stuff doesn't cost that much more than cheap stuff, but it performs better and lasts far longer.

Not sure you want to invest money in walking? That's fine. You can probably manage quite well with whatever you find in your closet. If you *must* spend money, buy shoes. Shoes can make the difference between walking for a lifetime or giving it up after about 15 minutes.

Kinds of Shoes

What you want here is comfort and adequate support for your feet. Chances are, you have shoes in your closet that will be fine, at least to get started. As you get into the habit of walking, find the kind of walking that most appeals to you, and have a better understanding of the kind of shoe you need, you might want to buy a new pair. When you are ready to shop, you have three styles of shoes to choose from—low (the shoe, like a sneaker, comes below your ankle), midheight (the upper comes up to the ankle), and high (as in a traditional hiking boot, the upper comes above your ankle).

Most people use low and midheight shoes. High shoes are used by people who do more serious hiking over rougher terrain. There is nothing to stop you from wearing these on any walk if they're comfortable for you, especially if you are walking on woodland paths or uneven country. You get more support with a higher shoe.

Shoe Design

Walking or hiking shoes are made with stiffer soles than running shoes are. The stiffer sole provides more support. The least expensive walking shoes are made with cut EVA midsoles (EVA stands for ethylene vinyl acetate, a plastic foam used in midsoles). Better shoes are made with a molded EVA midsole, a one-piece construction that provides more durability and lighter weight than the EVA cut from sheet stock. The best shoes—that is, the most durable—are made with a one-piece molded polyurethane sole and midsole. These shoes range from $50 to $100.

Three types of shoes designed with walking in mind.

The Athlete's Foot Wear Test Center in Naperville, Illinois, does an ongoing evaluation of both walking and running shoes. The walkers they use to test shoes run the gamut from casual walkers (people who walk under 2 miles daily for exercise) to moderate fitness walkers and performance walkers. They range in age from college age to senior citizens. The results of their tests make their way into the Athlete's Foot shops and are also published annually in the March/April issue of *Walking Magazine*. Among the newest refinements in walking shoes are performance shoes for people walking 4 miles an hour or faster (and using the quick steps and bent-arm swing of racewalking techniques) and walk/run shoes for those who do both.

Walking Magazine associate editor Sarah Bowen Shea says that the walk/ run category is "just exploding." The walk/run shoe has a more flared heel and more high-tech cushioning devices than the ordinary walking shoe. It's constructed of synthetic leather and a mesh upper, which makes it lighter and more breathable than most leather walking shoes. The walk/run shoe appeals especially to the considerable number of younger people, injured runners, and club burnouts who are coming to walking and are used to a better-looking, jazzier shoe.

COMFORT TIP Whatever praise the shoe reports give a shoe, if it is not comfortable for you, it is not the right shoe. The annual review in *Walking Magazine* is a good way of gathering information, but reading about a shoe is not a substitute for walking in it.

Shoes run the gamut in price from $45 to $125. Those *Walking Magazine* has reviewed for its '95 issue are similar to the '94 models, but Shea feels there will be some big differences in the '96 lines. "We hope shoe companies are going to be introducing the new materials and technologies into walking shoes as they do in their running shoe lines. In the next few years manufac-turers are going to realize just how important the walking shoe market is, and not just use recycled ideas. I think introductions are going to get more exciting. There's always some new technology, but it's going to become more cutting edge."

In other words, the walking shoes made by running shoe manufacturers have not yet reached the level of running shoes. An enormous amount of research and design has gone into running shoes for a long time, whereas walking shoes are a relatively recent addition for these companies. Dr. William Wilshire, a Bozeman podiatrist and podiatric surgeon, suggests that you may be better off buying running shoes than walking shoes. "There's a lot of hoopla in creating walking shoes," he says. "The shoe companies do a good job of making the need (for walking shoes) seem like it's there."

Or, as Tom Johnson, owner of the Bozeman Athlete's Foot, puts it, with running shoes "you get more bang for your buck." Running shoes, Mr. Johnson explains, offer more features for less money than those same features cost in a walking shoe. (While there is no reason not to walk in a running shoe, you wouldn't want to do the reverse.)

If the Shoe Fits . . .

Whatever is comfortable for you is adequate in a walking shoe. Good running shoes (training models with well-constructed soles), lightweight trail and hiking boots, and casual shoes with heavy rubber or crepe rubber soles are all appropriate for walking. If none of these are in your closet, and you are a first-time buyer of good walking shoes, make sure you get a shoe that fits well. The shoes should have arch supports and should elevate the heel a half to three quarters of an inch above the sole. Uppers should be made of materials that breathe, such as leather or nylon mesh.

However expert the salesperson is, you do have some responsibility here, too. Only you can tell how the shoe *feels*. Every shoe fits differently. Two shoes of the same size may fit radically differently. Each has different widths and

GET A GOOD FIT

1. Go to a store that specializes in sport shoes, with a staff trained to know what a proper fit means.

2. Tell the salesperson what you need, and get his expert opinion.

3. Have the salesperson measure your foot by checking your arch length and the foot's overall length.

4. Your feet may not be exactly the same size. Fit for the larger foot.

5. Try on several models.

6. Walk around in the shoes.

7. Make sure your toes fit comfortably into the front of the shoe.

8. Make sure your arch fits the shoe's arch and that the ball of your foot sits in the widest part of the shoe.

9. If you're going to be wearing heavier socks, try them on with the shoes (most stores have all kinds of socks available for this purpose).

different heel widths. Try on several. When you find a pair you like, try a couple of sizes in that shoe. All of this will help you be sure to get the right fit.

Most important—walk in the shoe. If it isn't comfortable in the store, it will *not* get comfortable with wear. Greg Caracciolo at Northern Lights says that the shoe must be comfortable from the first time you put it on. There is no break-in time on shoes this light.

Heavier people—whether overweight or just taller and larger—may crush midsoles faster than shorter, smaller people wearing the same shoe. These people should choose shoes with midsoles made of polyurethane rather than EVA. Polyurethane makes for a firmer midsole that takes longer to break down than EVA. (The midsole is the cushioning material between the insole and the shoe's bottom.) If you hit the ground with a heavy heel-strike, shoes with carbon-rubber outsoles provide the most durability.

Caring for Your Shoes

Most athletic-type walking shoes are made of leather, although many manu-facturers are moving away from leather and into the synthetics of running shoes, which are lighter, dry faster, don't absorb moisture, and are washable. (If you are among those people who can't wear synthetics because of heat problems with your feet, stick with leather.)

To wash synthetic shoes, use a liquid or a very mild dry detergent and wash on the cold cycle, then air-dry. Do not put the shoes in the dryer, as dryer heat damages the resilient foams used in both soles and liners. Leather shoes are not washable and should be waterproofed if you intend to walk through rain or on wet ground. If they do get wet, you'll find leather shoes will keep their shape better if you use a shoe tree—or stuff them with newspa-per—as they dry. Do *not* dry them in an oven or next to a heater, as they will get stiff and shrink and generally deteriorate.

Resoling works well with leather hiking boots because you probably spent some serious time breaking them in and the shoe uppers usually remain in good condition long after the soles are worn down. But, with the (relatively) cheap walking shoes now on the market, most people just buy new shoes when the sole is worn down. At this point the rest of the shoe is probably worn out, too. Tom Johnson says that most people tend to wear out their walking shoes in the toe first. You know it is time to buy new shoes when the toe is worn through or when the rubber on the outersole is worn so that you can see the midsole. Also, if you begin to feel aches and pains in your legs or back but have made no radical changes in your walking terrain, you may find that a new pair of shoes remedies the problem.

Socks

In an attempt to shower the walker (or runner) with comfort, some companies make special socks. One of the most popular designs is a sock that is thinner over the top of the foot and thicker on the bottom, where padding is most needed. Among the companies making this style is Thorlo, which offers a whole range, labeled "walking," "light trekking," "hiking," and "trekking." There are differences in thickness and color in each category, and these socks sell for between $8 and $9. Another brand offers a double-layered construction, which, according to the manufacturer, helps prevent blisters and keeps your feet cool and dry. For people with problems with blisters, polypropylene liners wick moisture, one of the causes of blisters, away from your feet. Wearing thin undersocks and heavier oversocks can also help prevent blisters. Still, the best blister prevention is adequately fitting shoes.

If you live where there are no running or outdoor stores (I can think of a few places in eastern Montana, for instance), you can order socks—and many other comforting things for your feet—from The Foot Store, P.O. Box 728, Johns Island, South Carolina 29457. Call 800-775-3668 to request a catalog.

© F-Stock/Caroline Wood

When it comes to walking, if your feet are happy, you're happy.

Handy Accessories

Packs

A rucksack ($25 to $150) is handy for holding the windjacket you've gotten too warm to wear, or for carrying a water bottle. Ultimate Directions in Rexburg, Idaho, makes fanny packs with external water bottles ($20 to $70), as well as a full-torso pack with external water bottle pockets ($150). Greg Caracciolo says people come into Northern Lights just to ask, "Do you have any Ultimates?" Fanny packs are wonderful for carrying water on a hot day.

© F-Stock/Allison Photography

Pedometers

Pedometers record the length of your walks. While this can be interesting for anyone, beginners might find it especially helpful to measure their distances. A pedometer can keep you from walking so far in one direction that you are unable to walk back with comfort. Some pedometers have a built-in clock, which allows you to calculate your walking rate without wearing a watch. Pedometers can record both the number of steps taken and the distance gone. If you are walking in new territory, a pedometer used in conjunction with a map can let you know how near you are to a specific point you want to reach. Pedometers are available at outdoor shops.

Walking Sticks

Some people carry a walking stick. A rather nice, old-fashioned touch, a walking stick provides extra support to lean on while walking on an incline, or if you stop to chat or to investigate a flower or a fallen leaf. You can also swing the stick along as you walk, which may help in the general rhythm of your walking. You can find a good stick yourself in the woods, or you can buy one. Some outdoor shops carry them, and wood carvers often sell them at craft fairs. Outdoor magazines carry ads for mail orders. The Poestenkill Hiking Staff Manufacturing Company at Box 300-WA, Poestenkill, NY 12140, will send you a free brochure showing their walking sticks.

Walking Poles

Some people use a ski pole or a modified ski pole as a walking stick. Some use two, which researchers at the University of Wisconsin at LaCrosse have recently discovered elevates both your heart and your mood. Poles manufactured specifically for walkers are made by the Exerstrider Corporation in Madison, Wisconsin, and NordicTrack in Minnesota. Exerstriders are rigid, like ski poles (and you size them as you would a ski pole), with an oversized cane tip at the end. NordicTrack's Powerpoles are collapsible and can be adjusted to different heights.

3

WALKING CORRECTLY

The human body has been engineered for walking. Its bony structure is made flexible with knee and ankle joints, arched feet, and the ball-and-socket joints that allow for an easy swing from the hips and shoulders. Neither arms nor legs are rigidly fixed to the spine, but can swing and pivot. The spine holds the body's trunk with its own jointed, flexible support. The body itself is superbly designed for carrying its own weight, while the distribution of that weight adds to the easy mechanics of walking. For instance, most of our weight is in the upper part of our bodies, which pulls us naturally forward. Forward progress is what walking is all about. Falling forward with each step, we are instantly caught by the second leg moving forward. It may sound awkward, but it works magnificently. More than half the muscles surrounding the bone structure are primarily engaged during walking. While we must learn some forms of locomotion, such as swimming or skiing, and make a conscious effort to do others, such as running or jumping, for any of us who are not disabled, walking is an unconscious act.

To walk, we put one foot in front of the other, and go. Our arms swing in opposition to our legs and in direct proportion to the speed at which we walk. Whether your posture is good or not, you are more or less forced into better posture by the activity of walking.

© F-Stock/Eric Sanford

For most adults, walking skills come easy and take little refinement.

It's Natural

All walking is instinctive, but there are ways to make this instinctive act more efficient. The more efficient your walk, the more comfortable your walking. You can walk longer and farther yet feel less tired. Walking efficiently is also natural. We simply need to lose the bad habits most of us have picked up along our various ways.

It is irrelevant whether you walk for exercise or pleasure or simply to get from the kitchen to the bedroom. Any way you do it, walking is as natural for humans as it is for birds to fly. Life, though, may become more enjoyable for those who walk farther than from the kitchen to the bedroom. For one thing, walking increases circulation and helps the body use oxygen more efficiently—which helps both the brain and the psyche to function more effectively (not to mention the benefits to skin, bowels, etc.) Working muscles drain off anxiety and anger. The rhythm of walking gets rid of the physical reactions to problems, allowing you to concentrate on the problems themselves. Writers, poets, and mathematicians traditionally go for walks to clear their heads. Then they get to work.

WALK EFFICIENTLY

1. Hold your head erect; keep your back straight and your stomach flat. Your toes should point straight ahead and your arms swing loosely at your sides.

2. As you step, land on the heel of your foot and roll forward to drive off the ball of the foot.

3. Take long, easy strides without straining for distance.

4. When walking up or down hills, or at a very fast pace, lean slightly forward.

5. Breathe. (It's okay to breathe with your mouth open if it's more comfortable for you.)

You can do all of this with other forms of exercise, too, of course, but walking is easiest. Walking, jogging, and hiking can all be forms of endurance training, a way to increase the fitness of your cardiorespiratory system, which not only affects your energy level but the length, pleasure, and quality of your life, as well. To effectively condition your cardiorespiratory system, you must make your heart work harder. This happens with such exercise as rapid walking, when your heart pumps more blood at a faster rate to provide the extra oxygen that muscles require during exercise. The heart, itself a muscle, must do this without becoming short of oxygen. As your fitness grows, your heart is able to increase the amount of oxygen it sends to your muscles, which in turn increases the functioning and efficiency of the heart. Jogging may do this faster than walking—although not by much—but you can get the same benefits from walking if you walk farther regularly and if your pace is brisk enough to increase both your breathing rate and heartbeat.

As a study at the University of Wisconsin has shown, you can also condition your cardiorespiratory system by adding poles to your walk. Because the poles tax your upper body, pole walkers increase their upper body endurance, reach their target heart rates at a slower walking speed, and feel happier to boot. Exercise physiologist John P. Porcari, who teaches in Wisconsin's master's program in adult fitness and cardiac rehabilitation, is one of the researchers involved in this study. He speculates that feeling

© Austrian Tourism Office

Walking poles are a great way to add a cardiorespiratory workout to your walks.

happier can be attributed to the release of endorphins—the chemicals that make you feel good—when you have a greater muscle mass working.

"You can only walk so fast," Porcari says, "so some people have a hard time getting into the training zone. You put poles in their hands and they walk at the same speed, but get greater benefit. If you walk 3 miles per hour without poles, you experience a 20% increase in heart rate and calories burned *with* poles."

WALK WITH POLES

Walking with poles is the same as walking without poles in that your leg and opposite arm move at the same time. The difference is that your arm movements are more exaggerated.

1. As your left leg moves forward, raise your right arm and reach forward to plant the pole in front of your body.
2. Meanwhile, push off the ground with the pole in your left hand and swing the arm back alongside your body until your hand ends up slightly behind your left hip. Your left arm is in its furthest rear position as your right arm reaches in its furthest forward position.
3. As you plant the pole in your right hand and push into the ground, move your left hand and right foot forward.

The whole movement is much more natural in execution than it sounds on paper!

Walking With Children

Because walking requires no particular skills and no particular speed, it is an ideal family event.

When children are very small, it's easy enough to put them in child carrier backpacks and be on your way. When they are old enough to walk, let them walk, although you'll have to gear your walks to their ability—shorter, slower, and more stops. Walking with a child requires being adaptable enough to change your plans. While most children can be *gently* persuaded that a view 10 minutes away at the top of a hill is a reward worth the walk, generally, when a child is ready to turn around, it is time to turn around, even if you must forego the view. The view will (more or less) always be there. The child will not. To force a child farther than he or she wants to go is to risk making the child hate walking forever.

Small children can become bored with just walking, so the more there is to explore along the way—the places animals live, the sounds animals make, a berry patch, the softness of woodland moss, a waterfall, the fish in a stream, a picnic with favorite foods, why the squirrel overhead is chattering so—the happier the child will be with the walk. For a child, a walk is *not* for exercise, but for adventure. The greater the adventure, the more a child will enter in, which provides an extraordinary opportunity for any accompanying adult. Children are so expert at adventure that to walk with a child is to learn about adventure. People obsessed with the idea of walking as exercise might do well to *borrow* a child, if they haven't one of their own, to reconnect with that sense of adventure.

© Photo Network/Myrleen Ferguson

If you want to do some exploring on your walk, you should take along an expert.

There are short walks throughout the world that can be done with young children, places where an hour on the path will lead to a wonderful view, a stream to wade or fish in, or a pretty mountain hut for an overnight stay. Walks might lead to a special place in the woods or meadows or to a special event—a campfire, a story-telling session, a view of animals, a place to pick berries, an historical site, where the story is still evident. If you have only one child, it can be a good idea to take along a friend of the child, as well. The two of them will make their own adventure out of the walk.

The idea here is for children to grow up thinking that walking is wonderful and that, as they grow, they continue to enjoy going for family walks. Forced walks will *not* do this. Childhood and the army are not the same. It's easy to turn a child off walking or skiing or backpacking or any other sport when you push for some kind of perfection rather than simply enjoying being where you are. A walk in the woods is much more about being in the woods than about going for a walk. For a child to grow up thinking an activity is fun, it has to *be* fun.

A CHILD SHALL LEAD THEM

Three-year-old Cory wandered a little behind Sarah, the woman leading a short hike for three small boys (and me) in the Maine woods. Cory, the youngest of the boys, was engrossed in some private adventure of his own until Sarah stopped at a patch of bright green moss and knelt to touch it. The two older boys touched it, too, but quickly, perfunctorily. Cory sat down on the path next to the moss and ran his hand across it; he pressed his hand down on the moss and into it, as if he would give himself entirely to this soft, yielding, gentle place in the forest. In the wonder on his face, I saw he had come to a magical place. Because I followed him, I had come here, too.

Packing for a Day Outing

How you pack for a day's outing depends on the season and the region of the world. Normally, a fanny pack or small daypack provides room enough for all you'll need. Take water, wherever you are. A quart will usually do, but you'll need more if you are walking in a hot season or hot place. Rain gear is usually wise because sudden storms can happen almost anywhere and will certainly happen if you are walking in mountains. Take a warm shirt, sweater, or light jacket to put on *before* you cool off when you stop for lunch. Don't forget lunch. And snacks. A small first-aid kit is a good idea. Other items you should bring along include a sun hat; sun cream; a bandanna to dip into a stream and cool you off, or to dry your feet after you've dipped them into a stream; a map if you are somewhere you've never been and are curious about more than simply walking; guidebooks to plants, animals, birds, butterflies, reptiles, or other wildlife that might be of special interest to you (don't pack a whole lot of these—they're heavy); binoculars, if you're interested in watching wildlife; a starmap and flashlight, if your walk is after dark; and an extra set of car keys.

Watching Wildlife

According to *Defenders of Wildlife*, an environmental organization whose chief focus is the protection of wildlife and wildlife habitat, wildlife watching may become the premier outdoor recreation activity of the '90s. While it seems that watching wildlife is an innocent enough occupation, in fact, there is a real danger of watching wildlife to death. That is, harassing animals by creating too great a disturbance can be critical to the point of being lethal. If your presence interrupts their normal behavior, they run serious risks. Watch, but watch from an appropriate distance. In any case, you'll see more of any animal's natural behavior and activity if you are sensitive to its need for space. You know you've come too close if animals stop feeding or stand up from a rest, if they start moving away from whatever it is they've been doing, or if they suddenly change their direction of travel. Too close, your presence can frighten an animal onto a road and into traffic, cause mothers and young to separate, distract animals from attention to their predators, or keep incubating or breeding birds off their nests, so that eggs or young birds become chilled and die. Your scent could lead predators to a nest or to young animals. In winter, when deep snow and cold make finding food difficult, disturbing animals may cause them to use up valuable energy they need to survive.

EARTH WATCH

You should never pick up wild baby animals. It is unlikely they are orphaned or abandoned. Their parents know where they are and will return to feed them.

You should not feed wild animals that you see on your walks. Animals that become accustomed to handouts may become aggressive around humans, with the result that they must be either moved out of the region or killed. Or they may not be able to tell the difference between the Twinkie and the plastic wrapping it, which can cause harm to their digestive systems. Those that hibernate may not gain enough body weight to survive the winter, while those that migrate may delay their trips too long to make them successfully.

© Courtesy of Corkscrew Swamp Sanctuary, Florida.

Observing wildlife through binoculars allows you to watch while keeping a healthy distance.

Developing an Environmental Awareness

Anyone using the earth has a responsibility to keep it pristine. It's so easy while walking to let a piece of Kleenex fall from your pocket or to mindlessly drop the wrapper from your candy bar. Don't. Litter not only makes the route less pleasant for the next walker, most of it isn't biodegradable, and all of it poses a threat to animals who may pick it up and ingest it or get caught in it. If you walk with pets on city streets, carry plastic bags to pick up after them. Stay on sidewalks or trails. There is no reason to walk across other people's property or cut new trails across fields or forests or mountains. New trails disturb plant life (and therefore animal life), and provide further pathways for erosion. Except in national parks, there is nothing wrong with picking berries or flowers along your way on public land (you may pick berries in national parks, if you eat them), so long as you leave plants the means to reseed. Don't pick those that are rare, or *all* of those that are not, and don't pull up any by the roots. Don't throw things into ponds or streams. Learn to listen to the sounds of water, wind, birds, and rustlings in the leaves; learn to smell the scent of seasons, streets, forests, meadows, oceans, and rain; learn to taste the rain and the heat of the sun. Know where you are and with whom you share it.

4

WALKING FITNESS AND SAFETY

How much time you put into
walking depends on what you expect to get out of it.

> . . . to be properly enjoyed, a walking tour should be gone upon
> alone. It you go in a company, or even in pairs, it is no longer a walking
> tour in anything but name; it is something else, and more in the nature
> of a picnic. A walking tour should be gone upon alone, because
> freedom is of the essence; because you should be able to stop and go
> on, and follow this way or that, as the freak takes you; and because you
> must have your pace, and neither trot alongside a champion walker,
> nor mince . . . you should be as a pipe for the wind to play upon.
> —Robert Louis Stevenson

Pacing Yourself

No one can tell you exactly how far or how fast to walk when you begin. Experiment. Start out by walking 20 minutes four or five times a week at a pace that feels comfortable. If you want to walk with someone whose pace is faster than yours, or whose legs are longer, or whose strength is greater, start out with him or her and then meet at the end, but don't try to walk at a pace that isn't your own. Once you begin a regular regimen of walking, if you get too tired or the walk seems too easy, reduce or lengthen your time accordingly. Some elderly people and some people who are ill may begin by walking a minute or two, resting a minute, then repeating the cycle until they tire.

As your fitness improves, gradually increase your time and pace so that after a month you are walking for 30 minutes. Your eventual goal may be to walk 3 miles (4.8 km) in 45 minutes, but walking is not about hurrying. There is no hurry to reach your goal.

Speed is less important than the time devoted to walking, although the more briskly you walk, the better your condition becomes. For anyone in reasonable health, 20 minutes is a kind of minimum. It takes 20 minutes for your body to begin experiencing the "training effects" of exercise.

To *find* the right pace, talk while you walk. This is one reason—Thoreau and Stevenson aside—that a walking companion is nice, but its okay to talk to yourself, too. If talking to yourself feels odd to you, take a dog. (If you don't have a dog of your own, borrow one, or see if your local humane society will let you walk their dogs.) If you can carry on a conversation while you're walking, you're okay. If you're too breathless to talk, you're going too fast. Your body tells you what it needs, if you will only listen. (You can also determine the proper walking speed by taking your pulse—see page 44—but I like the talking test better. It feels more natural to me.) Walking should be comfortable, so if you feel dizzy, pain, nausea, or any other odd symptoms, slow down or stop. If the problem continues, see your physician before you walk again.

It's a good idea to set up a specific walking schedule, as you would with any exercise (although the nice thing about walking is that if you hate the idea of exercise, you can still go for a walk). You don't *have* to walk for exercise. Even if you amble, you are doing more for your body than if you're sitting on the sofa. If you have been sedentary for a long time, start slowly, perhaps with a daily walk around the block or down to the corner for the newspaper. To begin, it doesn't matter how long the walk is or how long it takes. What matters is to walk at a comfortable pace, to walk regularly, and to enjoy it enough that you keep it up. Walk at the hour that feels best to you. If you do strenuous walking, you might prefer to walk before you eat, so your stomach won't hurt while you're walking, but casual walking after a meal (as opposed to sitting down with the daily paper or turning on the television) is a good goad to a less sedentary life. For those who have been sedentary, even a casual walk after a meal will help increase metabolism. The higher your metabolism, the more calories you burn.

© F-Stock/Kate Ryan

Dogs make great walking companions: They can help you find a comfortable pace and are great listeners.

WALKING FOR FITNESS

Spend the first 2 weeks walking a distance of 1 to 3 miles (1.6 to 4.8 km) at a slow pace (2-1/2 miles per hour). Walk an hour a day, for 5 days. By the third week, increase your mileage to 3 to 5 miles (4.8 to 8 km) at a moderate pace of about 3 miles per hour. Maintain your schedule of an hour a day for 5 days, and keep up this schedule for the next 3 weeks. From the sixth to the eighth weeks of your program, continue your distance of 3 to 5 miles (4.8 to 8 km), but increase your speed to a brisk walk of 3-1/2 miles per hour. You're still walking about an hour a day, 5 days a week. To increase your workout to peak fitness performance, you might, after 3 or 4 months of walking, add another mile, a hill or two, and another 2 days a week. As exercise, an hour a day for 5 days a week gets real results.

Getting Your Body Ready

For the serious walker, warming up is as important as it is for anyone engaging in any form of exercise.

Warming Up

Start your walk slowly. Five to ten minutes of easy strolling allows both your body temperature and your heart rate to rise gradually. The elevated heart rate speeds up your blood's circulation, quickens your breathing, and opens the airways in your lungs, all of which speed fuel to your muscles. The warmer your muscles are, the more quickly they can process that fuel. By warming up gradually, you can walk longer. Your muscles and tendons become more compliant, reducing the likelihood of injury.

Stretching

Walkers should also stretch. *Just* walking shortens and tightens the muscles in the back and backs of the legs, making you, in time, stiff and inflexible. Ideally, though, you should warm up for walking by walking, then stretch afterward, when your body is more flexible.

Stretching is easy and comfortable; it feels good while you're doing it and makes you feel good afterward. But bodies have different flexibilities. Some stretches that are easy or comfortable for one body will not be that way for another. Stretches that hurt should be avoided or done only moderately.

You can get the best idea of what a stretch should be by watching your cat or dog. They stretch out every part of themselves in a long, slow, luxurious way. Copy them. Do not bounce. Do not put pressure on your back. Do not overstretch. If you're not used to stretching, have someone watch you the first time or two through to make sure you're in the correct position. Or stretch in front of a mirror so you can check your own position.

The following few exercises are especially helpful for walkers. There are many others that can be beneficial, but these should provide a start.

CALF AND HIP STRETCH   Stand near a wall (or anything solid) and lean on it with your forearms, your head resting on your hands. Bend one leg and place that foot on the ground in front of you. Keep the other leg straight behind, with the heel firmly on the floor and your back straight. Keep your toes pointed straight ahead. Hold the stretch for 20 to 30 seconds, then repeat with your other leg.

CALF AND HIP STRETCH

CALF AND ACHILLES TENDON STRETCH

In the same position as for the calf and hip stretch, lower your hips downward as you slightly bend your knee. Your arms will also lower. Keep your back flat, your toes straight ahead, and your heel down. You will probably have to slide your foot slightly forward so that the space between your front and back foot is narrower than in the first exercise. Hold the stretch for 15 to 20 seconds, then repeat with your other leg.

CALF AND ACHILLES TENDON STRETCH

QUADRICEPS AND KNEE STRETCH

Stand with your right hand against a wall or bar for balance and hold the top of your right foot with your left hand, gently pulling your heel toward your buttocks. Hold for 15 seconds. Repeat with your other leg.

QUADRICEPS AND KNEE STRETCH

FRONT OF THE HIP, GROIN, AND HAMSTRINGS STRETCH   Place the ball of your foot on a secure support (wall, fence, table). Keep your back leg pointed straight ahead. Bend the knee of your forward leg as you move your hips forward. Hold for 30 seconds, then repeat with your other leg.

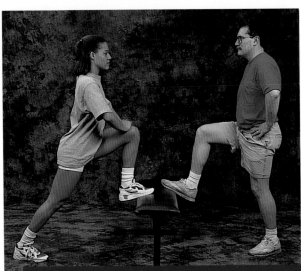

FRONT OF THE HIP, GROIN, AND HAMSTRINGS STRETCH

LOWER BACK, HIPS, GROIN, AND HAMSTRINGS STRETCH

Stand with your feet shoulder-width apart and pointed straight ahead. Slowly bend forward from the hips, *keeping knees slightly bent at all times*. (If your knees are straight, you put pressure on your lower back.) Relax your neck and arms. Continue to bend until you feel a slight stretch in the back of your legs. Hold for 15 to 25 seconds. Do not bounce, as bouncing contracts rather than stretches muscles. It does not matter how low you go. If you can touch the floor, fine. If the floor is too low, put your hands against a wall or table. The idea is to relax.

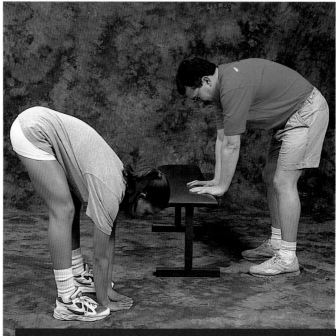

LOWER BACK, HIPS, GROIN, AND HAMSTRINGS STRETCH

UPPER BODY STRETCH

Stand with your feet about shoulder-width apart and toes straight ahead. Keep your knees slightly bent and reach both arms overhead, letting your hands connect. Bend slowly from your waist to the right until you feel the stretch. Hold 8 to 10 seconds. Move slowly back to center and bend slowly to the left. Hold 8 to 10 seconds.

UPPER BODY STRETCH

HAMSTRING STRETCH Sit with one leg straight but at an angle to your body. Bend your other leg with the sole of that foot slightly touching the inside of the other leg's thigh. Slowly bend forward from the hips toward the foot of the straight leg until you feel the slightest stretch. Hold for 20 seconds. When the stretching feeling decreases, bend a bit more forward from the hips. Hold for 25 seconds. Switch sides and repeat.

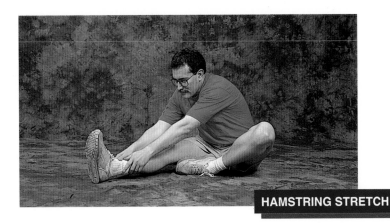

HAMSTRING STRETCH

CHEST OPENER Lace your fingers behind your back. Slowly turn your elbows inward while straightening your arms. Keep your chest out and your chin in. Lift your arms up behind you until you feel the stretch in your arms, shoulders, or chest. Hold an easy stretch for 5 to 15 seconds.

CHEST OPENER

Getting Intense

There is a certain intensity of exercise that must be reached to develop and maintain aerobic conditioning. Monitoring your heart rate is one way to gauge the intensity with which you are working. What you're looking for is a heart rate that ranges between 70% to 85% of your maximum heart rate. To estimate your maximum heart rate—that is, the maximum number of times your heart beats in 1 minute—subtract your age from 220. A 40-year-old woman, for instance, would have a maximum heart rate of 180 beats per minute. Her *target* heart rate would be between 126 (70%) and 153 (85%) beats per minute. You do not want to work at your maximum rate because doing so is uncomfortable and dangerous. If you're in good shape, you'll want to work toward the upper end of your target range. Older or sedentary people should exercise toward the lower end of their ranges. Keep in mind, though, that these numbers are just estimates and your threshold may be higher or lower. You can determine your heart rate by counting your pulse for 1 minute. To find your pulse, hold your palm up and place the index and middle fingers of your other hand on the wrist so that their tips lie on the thumb side. Once you feel your pulse, either count for a full minute or for 10 seconds and multiply by 6.

Walking Safely

Walking shouldn't be a difficult or dangerous activity, but people—through ignorance or carelessness—do things to make it harder and more dangerous. They walk when or where they shouldn't, they wear headphones or weights, or they ignore pain. If you follow a few basic, commonsense guidelines, walking will remain the pleasant pursuit it should be.

Take Off the Weights

Now and then you see people walking with ankle weights or wrist weights. According to Bozeman exercise physiologist Joy MacPherson, these devices have the potential for causing injury, as the ankle weights change your normal gait and the wrist weights change your arm movements. (Poles do not do this because your arms work in a natural, if somewhat exaggerated, swing.) Muscles in your legs, hips, or shoulders are all at risk with ankle and wrist weights, a risk MacPherson feels outweighs any benefits of increased muscle tone or caloric expenditure. The idea behind the weights is to add strength training to a cardiovascular workout. There *are* some ways to do this—for example, the aerobics circuits some health clubs offer, or the parcours tracks (running tracks with exercise stations along the way) laid out in some parks—but these are ways that separate the aerobics from the weight training, so that each is done alone, not in combination. Because walking is an exercise in which injury is extremely rare, it seems a shame to up the ante.

Take the Headphones Off

A gadget you do *not* need when walking outdoors is a Walkman. Whether you are on city or suburban streets or country roads, you should always be able to hear traffic. You need all your senses operating when you're walking so that you're alert enough to avoid trouble. The same is true if you are walking a woodland path. In many places, mountain bikers, horseback riders, and even bears and their cubs share the same trails with hikers. It's possible for you to stumble upon someone with little warning; therefore you'll want to know what is happening around you at all times. Hearing is a major clue to these things.

Beyond safety, part of walking outside is gathering the impressions of the natural world. Even in cities, you can hear birds and squirrels, the ripples of a stream, the slough of wind. These things and all the other sounds of forest and mountain and prairie and beach are even more pronounced outside of cities. If you're going to walk outside, enter *into* the outside. It works better if you do not separate yourself.

© F-Stock/Nancy Hoyt Belcher

The visual beauty of a walk is only half the picture; don't separate yourself from nature's sounds with headphones.

Don't Ignore Pain

People with foot problems will be happy to know that there are adaptations that can essentially remove the problems. Some of these adaptations are natural. According to Dr. Wilshire, compensatory adjustments are actually built into the mechanical nature of the foot. In other words, if one part of the foot doesn't function quite right, another part will take over. "This is all right to a certain point," Dr. Wilshire says, then adds, "this point would probably be pain." If there are serious problems with the foot's structure, such as flat feet or an extremely high arch, enough activity and weight are likely to produce foot problems somewhere down the road.

But just because your foot hurts doesn't necessarily mean there's something wrong with its structure. "About 90% of what I see are overuse problems," Dr. Wilshire says. "Most come on very slowly. Then it's a matter of how stubborn people are before they seek help."

If the problem is chronic and doesn't go away even after you buy a good pair of shoes, it's probably time to see a podiatrist. Chronic problems are generally caused by an abnormal foot structure, something you cannot treat yourself. A podiatrist will likely suggest the most conservative step—orthotics, which are made specifically for your feet from casts done while your foot is in a neutral, non–weight-bearing position. (You can buy shoe inserts or out-of-the-box devices—also often called "orthotics"—but they are basically a waste of money.)

HEALTH TIP   There are various things to try to help yourself before going to a podiatrist: a better pair of shoes, an arch support, a pain reliever, rest. Stay off what hurts until it feels better.

The orthotics made by a podiatrist compensate for the structure of your foot, making your foot function more normally by essentially tricking your foot into thinking it is wholly on the ground. The foot that doesn't do this on its own may be *pronated*, which is when you stand with the big toe down and the little one up (the foot rolls excessively inward as you walk), or *supinated* (or *underpronated*, a word used often in shoe shops), which is the opposite—when the little toe is on the ground, the big toe is up and the foot rolls excessively outward.

Pronation, to a point, is actually a built-in shock absorber, but either of these things in excess can affect your entire skeleton, causing you knee and back problems in addition to giving you feet that hurt. Orthotics control pronation and supination, so, while they are not cheap (they run around $300), they are considerably easier to get than new feet. As Dr. Wilshire suggests, "If you have a foot problem that doesn't go away on its own, you need to see a doctor. If you *need* an orthotic, you need a prescription, one custom-made for your foot."

How do you know if you've got a foot problem? "Pain," Dr. Wilshire answers. "Pain is never normal, it's never good, and you should never ignore it."

© Unicorn/Charles E. Schmidt

Foot pain should not be ignored, so listen to your feet.

CONSUMER TIP   If you wear orthotics, take them with you to the store when buying shoes. Shoes fit differently with orthotics in them than without.

Some shoes are built to compensate for overpronating by providing enough arch support and firm inner-foot midsoles. For the underpronating foot, which is usually very rigid, the appropriate shoe is usually a nonsupportive, cushy shoe with a curved or semicurved last. (A *last* is the mold around which the shoe's upper is shaped. It determines the shape and fit of the shoe.) The underpronated foot can't absorb shock naturally, so the shoe must do it.

If you overpronate, your shoe will be worn more on the inside of the sole than the outside. If you underpronate, the outside of the sole will be most worn. If you're not sure what your foot does, the salesperson can usually tell by looking at your usual walking shoes or at your feet as you stand.

If you are not a candidate for podiatrist-made orthotics but would like as much comfort as you can get, an insole made by Superfeet In-Shoe Systems, Inc., is worth investigating. Like orthotics, these insoles are fitted in a non–weight-bearing position by a Superfeet technician. The technician molds a foot bed to your foot, providing you with a close to perfect fit and the good foot stability that comes with proper fit. Superfeet makes no claim to being an orthotic, warning potential customers not to confuse Superfeet products with corrective orthotics made by licensed podiatrists. Their literature specifically says, "although Superfeet products provide dramatic support and comfort, they are not a substitute for the medically supervised correction of chronic foot conditions." For information about Superfeet, write them at P.O. Box 186, Custer, Washington 98240, or call them at 800-634-6618. These inserts cost from $50 to $100, depending on the particular type of insert, which depends on the use of the particular shoe.

Avoid Blisters

Foot blisters result when skin rubs against a sock or shoe. This can happen if your shoes don't fit properly, if your socks are wrinkled or lumpy, or if the weather is very hot. Blisters can occur even if you are wearing the right shoes and socks but your shoes are improperly laced. If you feel a hot or otherwise uncomfortable spot on your foot, stop at once and adjust your sock or lacing. If there is already a red area, molefoam (moleskin) applied over it often relieves the discomfort and prevents further problems. If you have a spot that blisters regularly, put the thickest molefoam you can find over it before you go out. If you already have a blister, put molefoam *around* it, cutting out a hole for the blister.

TREAT BLISTERS PROPERLY

Leave small blisters alone. If they are large, or about to pop, they should be opened.

1. Wash the area with soap and water and sterilize a needle with a match.
2. Insert the needle under the skin just beyond the blister's edge, then pass it into the blister.
3. Press the fluid out gently and put a sterile bandage over the spot.
4. A blister that has already broken should be treated like any open wound. Wash it thoroughly and apply a sterile dressing.
5. If the blister looks infected, use a local antibiotic.

While blisters are a nuisance for most of us, people with diabetes can have special foot problems that may even become limb threatening. Because people with diabetes may not even feel a foot blister, they may easily just keep on walking their way into serious complications. Those with diabetes should consult their doctor before beginning regular walking. Walking can be truly helpful for people with diabetes, but because such things as the timing of walks and meals and the kind of weather you walk in can be crucial, talking to your doctor about it is important. For those seriously threatened by blisters, the doctor may prescribe a different form of exercise.

Know Your Environment

Some safety rules are common sense; others may be of particular urgency in particular areas. Perhaps the most important information is to know where you are. In a city, know your neighborhood(s). If you're in rural or wild country, be alert to everything from weather changes to sounds to unusual movement. In an urban environment, walk during daylight or, if you must walk at night, carry some sort of protective spray. Day or night, if you have any trepidations at all, walk with a companion—human, or canine (not a Lhasa apso!). Stay in the middle of sidewalks away from doorways. If someone follows you, go into a shop, *not* into your apartment building or house. Obey traffic signs at busy intersections, even if they interfere with your rhythm.

DOG RENTAL

The Project Safe Run Foundation is the brainchild of Oregon's Shelley Reecher, who trains and supplies protection dogs for women runners, walkers, and campers in several Pacific Northwest cities. In the 12 years of the nonprofit, all-volunteer program's existence, more than 14,000 runs have been made without a single assault on the woman with dog. The dogs are taught basic obedience and whom to obey. They will not be lured by treats, and they know when, where, and how to do protection work. For more information, or to find out how you can bring Project Safe Run to your city or arrange to have your own dog trained by the PSR Foundation's sister corporation, Canine Training and Security, write them. The address is:

Project Safe Run
c/o P.O. Box 22234
Eugene, Oregon 97402.

On rural walks, walk facing traffic, carry water to drink, and bring along a watergun or stick or stones to ward off dogs. A few rocks hurled toward—but not *at*—a dog will usually send it running. But be careful. Most dogs are not mean, but their instinct is to chase anything moving fast, which is one reason walking is better for your health than running. A firm *stay* or *go home* can also work well.

When walking wildland trails, stick to the trails. Let someone know your route and estimated time of return. Be aware of the others with whom you share the environment. You do not want to walk between any mother animal and her young. When walking on beaches, know tide schedules. Tides come in rapidly in some regions. In bear country, carry pepper spray on a belt in one of the holsters specially made for it. It will not help you if it is in your pack. (This is also true on city streets.) Always carry water.

If you're used to walking on a particular surface—pavement, earth, sand—be aware that changing to any other surface will affect how you walk. Your stride and pace will change. The effect on your whole body will be different. Do not expect to feel the way you feel on your usual routes. The same thing happens when you change climates, or when the seasons change.

In extreme heat, your body is quickly depleted of water and minerals, and you must drink *before* you get thirsty. While a short walk will probably only make you long for a swimming hole, strenuous exertion at hot temperatures can cause heat exhaustion. Faintness, nausea, palpitations, sweating, and headaches are the usual symptoms. Rest. Drink fluids. Untended, heat

© Photo Network/Pinkerton-Arend

Stopping regularly for water is not only healthy, it's a great way to drink in the scenery.

exhaustion can lead to heat stroke. Confusion, staggering, and eventual coma are possibilities here. Sweating is reduced or absent and your body temperature soars up to 105 or 106 degrees. At these times, the body *must* be immersed in a cold stream or lake as soon as possible or medical attention sought.

In extreme cold, breathing is difficult because it hurts to inhale frigidly cold air. A scarf wrapped over your nose and mouth, or a balaclava, can help warm the air before it gets to your lungs. Spenco makes a cold-air mask that looks funny but helps warm and moisten inhaled air in a cold, dry environment. The mask costs $9.95 from The Foot Store (call 800-775-3668).

The combination of physical exhaustion and wet clothing make hypothermia a real possibility in even less than extremely cold weather. If you're planning a long walk, make sure you have waterproof clothing and high-calorie food for frequent snacks.

Extreme humidity is just plain uncomfortable. You probably won't overdo exercise under these conditions simply because you won't feel like overdoing it. Any time you pay attention to what your body is telling you, you are probably right.

5

THE BEST PLACES TO WALK

Being a walker opens up a seemingly infinite number of options for vacations or day-long outings. It makes visits to cities more alive; while on back roads, beaches and woodland, mountain, and meadow paths, you have a chance to see rural life, wildlife, and the life of small villages off the beaten track. In much of the world, inns, guesthouses, and mountain refuges offer you, as a walker, a hearty meal, a place to sleep, and a chance to meet other people with whom you share at least one thing in common—you have all walked to get there.

Eight Great Urban Walks in North America

New York

© Photo Network/Henryk T. Kaiser

Walk up the east side of Fifth Avenue from 59th Street to 103rd Street with its old mansions, townhouses, and museums (if you stop at each museum, this walk of about 2-1/2 miles [4 km] takes about a week and a half). Central Park is across the street. If you're up for another 2-1/2 miles, walk back down along the park and perhaps stop off at the quite extraordinary zoo.

San Juan, Puerto Rico

© Courtesy of Puerto Rico Tourism Company

From the Little Plaza of the Nuns, walk along the two remaining step streets in the city—the delightful Caleta del Hospital, lined with pots of plants and flowers and ice-cream colored houses, and the Calle San Sebastian (turn right) to the San Jose Plaza. The plaza leads to a park providing entrance to El Morro, the old (and very Old-World) fortress built to protect the island against invasion.

Milwaukee, Wisconsin

© Courtesy of Greater Milwaukee Convention/Visitors Bureau

Starting at the Milwaukee County Historical Society Museum at North Third Street and West Kilbourne Avenue, a walk of about 3 miles (4.8 km) through Juneautown, the city's historic section, leads you past interesting buildings, among them City Hall (a marvel of Flemish Renaissance architecture) and the rather newer Eero Saarinen War Memorial Center, as well as the 19th-century German facades of restaurants and shops.

Québec

©Yves Tessier/CuQ Comm

With its old, narrow, cobbled streets and open squares and the thick stone of its buildings, walls, and ramparts, Québec is one of the few cities in North America that offers a walker a sense of this continent's old civilization. Old Québec was the first North American city included on UNESCO's World Heritage list. The Tourism Office has mapped out a 2-1/2 hour walking tour with views of the St. Lawrence River, the Laurentians, and the Lower City.

Seattle, Washington

© Courtesy of East King County Convention Bureau

Starting at Pioneer Square, walk through Seattle's history and along its waterfront to Waterfront Park. Just east of the park, between Pike and Pine streets, is the Pike Place Market, where you'll find as large a selection of foods, flowers, clothing, and various treasures to choose from as anywhere else in the West.

Ketchikan, Alaska

© Ketchikan Alaska Visitors Bureau/Jeff Isaac Greenberg

In a couple of hours, you can walk most of this town built on steep, rocky slopes rising up out of the sea. Starting at the Visitors' Bureau on the waterfront, walk north along Mission Street, cross Ketchikan Creek on a footbridge (from which you can watch schools of salmon during spawning season) to arrive at Creek Street, a boardwalk on pilings with wonderful old wooden buildings. Retracing your steps over the footbridge, walk down Dock Street to Bawden Street to Park Avenue and the Grant Street Trestle, the only remaining example of all Ketchikan's early walkways and streets. Follow (mostly) the river to the Totem Heritage Center, which offers an insight into the original civilization of this region.

San Francisco, California

© San Francisco Convention and Visitors Bureau/David Weintraub

The Golden Gate Promenade, from Victorian Square (part of the Golden Gate National Recreation Area) to the Fort Point National Historic Site is a round-trip of about 6 miles (about 10 km). From Victorian Square, a short walk leads you to the Hyde Street Pier, Fisherman's Wharf, and Ghirardelli Square, where the marvelous array of shops and restaurants may cut down your promenading miles considerably.

San Antonio, Texas

© San Antonio Convention and Visitors Bureau/Al Rendon

Start at the Visitors' Information Center across the Plaza from the Alamo, then head for the Alamo and west on Crockett Street to the Paseo del Rio, the city's famous River Walk. Pedestrian walkways line both sides of this arm of the San Antonio River as it runs through a canyon about 20 feet (7 m) below the downtown street level. Start your walk hungry, because along with the beautiful flowers, you'll find some wonderful cafes.

Travel Ready for Anything

If your plans include leaving your own locality, check local weather conditions with walking clubs or tourist associations that deal with the outdoors. The weather may be radically different from yours at home. (I have walked in snowstorms in July in the Rockies, the Alps, and New Hampshire's White Mountains and in May in the Utah desert.) High places are frequently wet, cold, and foggy when the lowlands are in sun—or vice-versa. High-altitude sun is far more penetrating than the sun at sea level. Low-lying places may be boggy, marshy, or extremely humid. Carry a small rucksack on your back so you can take off or put on whatever clothing is necessary during the course of your walk.

Walking the U.S.

Some of America's easiest and most enjoyable trails are on old canal towpaths and railroad beds, both of which are full of the history of this country.

CANAL TOWPATHS

Who can look at a canal where water still runs and not see upon it that erstwhile, vital, lusty life of the canals—the big, freight-laden boats carrying entire families; dogs and chickens scampering over decks where small children were tied to keep them from falling overboard while boat-borne entrepreneurs selling food and fabric, medicine, books, whiskey—and everything else necessary for life—plied the canals to serve them. The greater efficiency and speed of railroads usurped most of the canal's work, but the spirit of those days still permeates the air around their waters.

The towpaths, built for the mule teams that pulled the boats, were also the province of professional "path walkers." Their job was to keep the canal flowing by trimming errant vegetation along the canal, repairing slides started by rain, filling in holes made by burrowing animals, and building up any part of the bank that had been washed away.

Towpaths are splendid places for today's kind of path walkers. Some old towpaths have been reclaimed specifically for walking. Others—the hundreds of miles along dried-up, abandoned canals once used by miners for hydraulic sluicing, especially in California and Georgia—can be easily walked without being officially reclaimed. Bushwhacking through the woods, for instance, you may come upon an old canal lock. For anyone ready to explore, historic canal sites undiscovered for a hundred years or more await you.

Like the railroads that followed them, canals passed through urban areas, which means it is generally easy for people living in cities to get to them. Of all the canal towpaths, the most gloriously developed is that of the Chesapeake and Ohio, which spans 185 miles (296 km) from Cumberland, Maryland, to Georgetown in Washington, DC. Although none of the other towpaths come near this length, they all provide scenic, level walks. The miles you walk are your own choice. You don't risk boredom by turning around and going back the way you came because everything is always different from the opposite direction.

The best source for further information is the American Canal and Transportation Center, 809 Rathton Road, York, Pennsylvania 17403. This organization acts as a sort of clearinghouse for all canal-centered activity and puts considerable energy into both trying to make parks out of old canals and encouraging the study and mapping of canals. Among their publications is one meant specifically for walkers, the *Towpath Guide to the Chesapeake & Ohio*, a mile-by-mile directory for the canal's entire length (cost is $15). They also publish *Towpaths to Tugboats* ($7), a history of canal building throughout the world. In the section called "Historical Canal Preservation," you'll find information about a number of canals in the northeastern U.S. where restored sections of old canals provide easy walking. The Center will send you a list of its other canal publications, as well as a list of other canal-related organizations that can provide information about canals in areas that interest you.

ABANDONED RAILROADS

Walking the rails is a time-honored tradition—made somewhat easier, perhaps, by the lack of rails. Ties and tracks have been removed from many abandoned railroad rights-of-way, and these have been specifically designated for the use of walkers, bicyclists, joggers, backpackers, horseback riders, and cross-country skiers.

The trails are gentle and easy. Railroads were built on level ground or with long, gentle grades so heavy engines could make it uphill. Access to the trails is also generally easy because the rights-of-way cut across urban regions as well as through countryside. The trails themselves provide open space—albeit often long and narrow open space—in some otherwise developed areas. By the 1970s, as open space in urban areas became a diminishing commodity while the populations of urban areas increased, it became obvious that open space for recreation was increasingly necessary. Turning abandoned railroad rights-of-way into trails was an ideal way to meet the need.

Under a federal Rails-to-Trails Grant Program, nine projects received grant money to build trails. These, combined with the few pioneering trails

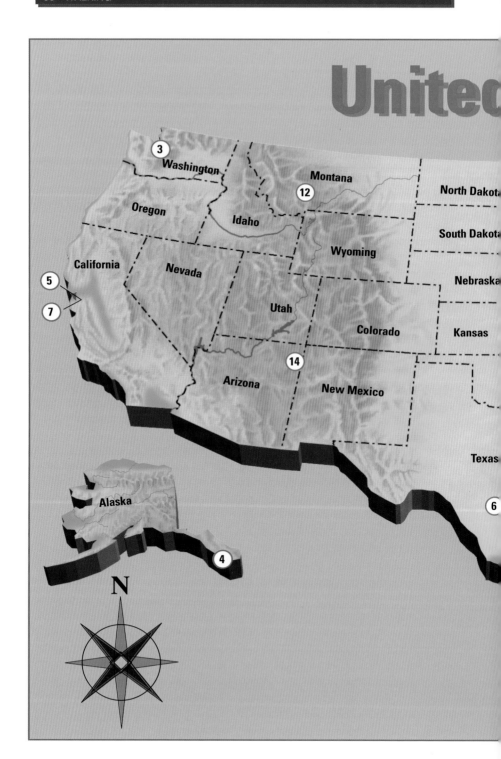

1	New York	8	Cuyahoga Valley National Recreation Area
2	Milwaukee	9	Indiana Dunes National Lakeshore
3	Seattle	10	Gateway National Recreation Area
4	Ketchikan	11	Black Rock Forest
5	San Francisco	12	Bear Trap Canyon
6	San Antonio	13	Corkscrew Swamp Sanctuary
7	Golden Gate National Recreational Area	14	Canyon de Chelly National Monument

already in place—the Illinois Prairie Path, Wisconsin's Elroy-Sparta Trail, and Seattle's Burke-Gilman Trail—have also provided the inspiration for the development of many trails along railroad rights-of-way in other places—the mile-long stretch near my house in Montana, for instance, where I walk my dog each morning. The trails, most of them helped along with the advice and expertise of the Rails-to-Trails Conservancy, have been built and opened and are maintained under the auspices of local, state, or county agencies.

The paths are a link to America's history, souvenirs of that lost age when the railroad steamed its glorious way across the continent, connecting civilization with wilderness and opening up the future. What an invitation to adventure was the whistle of the train speeding through the night fields beyond my house! How far I traveled as a child lying in bed, listening, waiting nightly for the whistle. Now, when walking an old rail bed, as I come across bridges and tunnels, often left exactly as they were over the trackless path, I feel strongly the journeys that beckoned in that whistle's call.

The tunnels, incidentally, are real havens on hot summer days as you make your way through country and town. The rail beds themselves may lead you past abandoned stations, overgrown farms, or a ghost town or two. You

An old railroad bridge—part of Michigan's Rails-to-Trails project.

might come upon one of the old station houses given a new life. Some have been recycled into restaurants, shops, cultural centers, or trail headquarters.

From a very local start in the mid-1960s, when people, seeing abandoned railroad tracks in their own communities, figured they might as well use the right-of-way to walk on, there are today 680 miles (1,088 km) of rail trails. These miles, divided among 557 trails in 45 states, are walked by millions of people a year.

The Rails-to-Trails Conservancy publishes a directory—*500 Great Rail Trails*—that lists rail trails around the country, including start and end points, mileage, location, trail surface, allowable uses, and the trail manager's name for more information. The directory is available from the Rails-to-Trails Conservancy, 1400 Sixteenth Street NW, Suite 300, Washington, DC 20036, for $9.95 for nonmembers. (The cost is $7.95 for members, of whom there are currently 53,000. Membership costs $18 and buys you a quarterly newsletter and discounts on publications and merchandise.) The directory will eventually be replaced with regional guides that will include maps, descriptions, and information on facilities along the corridors. The first of these is a guide to rail trails in the Great Lakes region. The guides will also be available through the Conservancy, as well as through booksellers.

THE NATIONAL TRAILS SYSTEM

The National Trails Systems Act authorized four kinds of trails: National Recreation Trails in or near urban areas; National Scenic Trails, such as the 2,000-mile (3,226-km) Appalachian Trail from Maine to Georgia and the 2,600-mile (4,193-km) Pacific Crest Trail from Canada to Mexico; National Historic Trails such as the 1,170-mile (1,872-km) Nez Perce National Historic Trail, or the Trail of Tears, which follows the 19th-century forced march of 16,000 Cherokee Indians from their homes in the southeast to the Oklahoma Territory; and connecting side trails. Recreation Trails can be designated by the Secretaries of the Interior and Agriculture. Scenic and Historic trails are established by Congress.

National Scenic Trails are *intended* to be continuous, on-the-ground trails, but there are missing links on most of the trails. In some places trails exist but have not yet been certified as part of the system. In other places there are no trails and you must figure out connecting roads to walk. National Historic Trails are more like beads on a string in which major historic sites are linked but not necessarily connected. The routes of Historic Trails are largely over roadways or, in the case of the Lewis & Clark Trail, over water (a logical turn of events since the original trails generally followed the easiest route to wherever they were going). But there are off-road paths at various points along most of these routes, so they all make interesting drive-and-walk trips. Well, almost all. The Iditarod National Historic Trail is basically usable only during Alaska's 6-month winter when rivers and tundra are frozen. While you *could* follow it on skis or snowshoes, it may be best done with a dog sled.

The National Scenic Trails, on the other hand, offer any walker the possibility of a few hours' walk, or a walk of months. Some people spend whole lifetimes doing an entire trail in bits and pieces, a week or two at a time. Some trails are more physically challenging than others, although sections along all of them vary in difficulty. Check out the terrain with the appropriate agency before starting out.

National Recreation Trails, which range in length from .1 mile on Arkansas' Buckeye Trail and Florida's Discovery Trail to the 365-mile (584-km) Seaway Trail in New York, include almost as great a variety of trail types, uses, topography, history, and physical challenge as they do length. These kinds of trails exist all across the country. Some are open year-round, others seasonally. Many have been designed for wheelchair use. A register listing these trails by state, noting seasons open, types of uses, trail surface, and length and the administrating agency from whom you can get more information is available from the U.S. Government Printing Office, Superintendent of Documents, P.O. Box 371954, Pittsburgh, Pennsylvania 15250. Ask for stock # 024-005-01113-7. The cost is $6. As a walker, I find this among my most useful references.

For further information on the whole National Trails System, contact the National Trails System Branch, National Park Service (782), P.O. Box 37127, Washington, DC 20013-7127. Or call 202-343-3780.

There are also urban areas maintained by the National Park Service that retain some remnant aura of wild in which to go for a walk.

Golden Gate National Recreation Area in California consists of 73,121 acres (29,614 ha) along shoreline areas of San Francisco and Marin and San Mateo counties. Designated a Biosphere Reserve in 1988, this region of ocean beaches, redwood forest, lagoons, and marshes provides natural habitat of world importance. For information: Golden Gate National Recreation Area, Ft. Mason, Building 201, San Francisco, California 94123.

Cuyahoga Valley National Recreation Area, Ohio, consists of 32,524 acres (13,172 ha) extending about 20 miles (32 km) along the Cuyahoga River from the southern edge of Cleveland to the northern edge of Akron. The old Ohio and Erie Canal ran through the region, and the towpath is still there to walk. For information: Cuyahoga Valley National Recreation Area, 15610 Vaughn Road, Brecksville, Ohio 44141.

Indiana Dunes National Lakeshore, Indiana consists of 13,844 acres (5,606 ha) of sand dunes, bogs, marshes, swamps, and prairie remnants along Lake Michigan, 60 miles (96 km) east of Chicago and exactly between Gary and Michigan City—in other words, smack in the middle of one of the

NATIONAL SCENIC TRAILS

Appalachian Trail

2,144 miles (3,430 km) from Maine to Georgia.

For information:

Appalachian Trail Conference
P.O. Box 807
Harpers Ferry,
West Virginia 25425

National Park Service
Appalachian Trail Project Office
c/o Harpers Ferry Center
Harpers Ferry,
West Virginia 25425
Or call 304-535-6278

Continental Divide Trail

3,200 miles (5,120 km) from Canada to Mexico.

For information:

Continental Divide
Trail Society
P.O. Box 30002
Bethesda, Maryland 20814

Forest Service, Northern Region
Federal Building
P.O. Box 7669
Missoula, Montana 59807
Call 406-329-3150

Forest Service
Rocky Mountain Region
P.O. Box 25127
Lakewood, Colorado 80225
Call 303-275-5350

Florida Trail

1,300 miles (2,080 km) from Big Cypress National Preserve in South
Florida to Gulf Islands National Seashore in the western panhandle.

For information:

Florida Trail Association
P.O. Box 13708
Gainesville, Florida 32604
Call 904-378-8823 or
800-343-1882 (Florida only)

Forest Service
National Forests in Florida
227 N. Bronough Street, Suite 4061
Tallahassee, Florida 32301
Call 904-942-9300

Ice Age Trail

1,000 miles (1,600 km) through Wisconsin from Lake Michigan to the St. Croix River.

For information:

Ice Age Park and
Trail Foundation
P.O. Box 422
Sheboygan, Wisconsin 53082

National Park Service
Ice Age National Scenic Trail
700 Rayovac Drive, Suite 100
Madison, Wisconsin 53711
Call 608-264-5610

Natchez Trace Trail

110 miles (176 km) divided into four segments that follow the historic Natchez Trace from Natchez, Mississippi, to Nashville, Tennessee.

For information:

National Park Service
Natchez Trace Parkway
RR 1, NT-143
Tupelo, Mississippi 38801
Call 601-842-1572

Natchez Trace Trail Conference
P.O. Box 6579
Jackson, Mississippi 39282
Call 601-373-1447

North Country Trail

3,200 miles (5,120 km) from New York's Adirondack Mountains to the Missouri River in North Dakota.

For information:

North Country Trail
Association
P.O. Box 311
White Cloud, Michigan 49349
Call 616-689-1912

National Park Service
North Country National
Scenic Trail
700 Rayovac Drive, Suite 100
Madison, Wisconsin 53711
Call 608-264-5610

Pacific Crest Trail

2,638 miles (4,220 km) from Canada to Mexico.

For information:

Pacific Crest Trail Conference
P.O. Box 2514
Lynnwood, Washington
98036-2514

Forest Service
Pacific Northwest Region
P.O. Box 3623
Portland, Oregon 97208
Call 503-326-3544

Forest Service
Pacific Southwest Region
630 Sansome Street
San Francisco, California 94111
Call 415-705-2889

Potomac Heritage Trail

700 miles (1,120 km) along the Potomac River in Washington, DC, Maryland, Virginia, and Pennsylvania. The 184-mile (294-km) long C & O Towpath (see canal towpaths, p. 64) is part of this trail.

For information:

Potomac Heritage Trail
Association
5229 Benson Avenue
Baltimore, Maryland 21227

National Park Service
National Capital Region
Land Use Coordination
1100 Ohio Drive SW
Washington, DC 20241
Call 202-619-7027

most industrial sections of the U.S. Nearby are steel mills, railways, highways, and a large port, which make this oasis of wildness some very special land. For information: Indiana Dunes National Lakeshore, 1100 N. Mineral Springs Road, Porter, Indiana 46304.

Gateway National Recreation Area consists of 26,310 acres (10,655 ha) of park land—beaches, marshes, islands, and various historic structures, all in unconnected pieces—surrounding the entrance to New York Harbor. For information: Gateway National Recreation Area, Headquarters Building 69, Floyd Bennett Field, Brooklyn, New York 11234.

Courtesy of New Zealand Tourism Board

Even relatively short walks can get you to some amazing places.

A FEW SHORT WALKS IN THE U.S.

I have walked in every state in the United States where there are mountains, and a few without. Many of my walks are backpacking trips because I like being able to get as far as possible inside wild country. But a walk of a few hours or a day is also wonderful. I relish the freedom a short walk gives me to leave a heavy pack behind and, in fact, *any* walk that gets me more than half an hour away from the road usually provides me with both a sense of real wildness and solitude.

Even a short walk in the woods is a chance just to walk, to look at wildflowers or birds, to find the tracks of animals, perhaps to find the animals, to enter nature as fully as you can. Nature is made up of grizzly bears and sequoias, but it is made up even more of spiderwebs and star flowers. You have to go slowly and gently to see them. It takes time to peer beneath things.

© F-Stock/David Stocklein

A walk allows you to enter into nature—to peer beneath things.

In forests, shy wildflowers like violets or Canada dogwood or trillium—and probably a hundred others—hide beneath and behind this year's green, while some fungi—like wondrous Indian pipe—lie hidden beneath dead leaves piling up forever on the forest floor. Inside the cracks in rocks, tiny, mighty wildflowers grow, their roots reaching far down for a nurturing place, their small petals able to withstand brutal wind and storm.

Each tree in the forest is an individual, the color and texture of its bark as special as the shape and color of its leaves. Walk your path through all the seasons and watch a tree through the seasons—from its first tiny buds to its flowering to the unfolding of its leaves, gaining almost visibly day by day in color and size and richness. Watch the colors change. Each kind of tree has its own colors, its own timing. Some hold insistently on to dried brown leaves throughout the winter, when the winter limbs against the sky define your tree as it can never be defined in other seasons.

Crush the needles of an evergreen between your fingers; scratch the bark to see if it smells the same as the needles; learn the tree from its scent. Look at the needles of various evergreens. See how different the pines are from the firs, the spruce, the cedar. Stop walking long enough to sit a while beneath a tree and wonder about its roots.

NORTHEAST: Black Rock Forest

This walk is a favorite among my shorter walks. When I lived in New York I often hiked in Black Rock Forest, a 45-minute drive from my apartment in the city. I loved that walk in all seasons, but summer may have been my favorite time because the scent of the pines is so strong then. For me, that has always seemed a kind of ultimate summer scent.

It is a short climb from the trailhead on Mine Hill Road (reached from Route 17 to Mountainville) to a junction with the Sackett Mountain Trail which, soon afterward, joins the Schunemunk-Storm King Trail—the trail to Black Rock. The walk is about 3 miles (4.8 km) one way, sheltered from the sun for much of the way by the thick green of the trees in full leaf. In summer, there is almost always a gentle breeze to cool the woods. In early summer, the laurel is in bloom. I remember well walking through a forest that, at waist level, was entirely pink.

At the top of the ridge above Sutherland Pond, a short side trail veers off to Echo Rock (at 1,400 feet; 426 m). Never one to waste an opportunity to sit during a walk, I always stopped at Echo Rock to indulge in the views of the pond and the hills to the south. The rock gives you a wonderful sense of how high you've come above the valley. In the distance, between and above the hills to the south, hawks soar and swoop. The water below is clear, hypnotizing, as the sun jumps, sparkling, upon it, the sun's motion controlled by the movement of water and the wavering leaves of trees edging it.

Walking again, heading toward the pine woods, the path is always hot in summer. The high trees here are far enough back that the sun reaches the path fully. But so does air, so I could immerse myself in the air and sun and golden heat. Even before I reached the pines, their scent came out to meet me. Stepping inside the woods is like hitting a cold patch of water in a warm lake. Years of pine needles make the path soft. I remember the woods as deeply silent. In the heat of the day, I never heard the sound of a bird.

However hot the day, there is always a wind on top of Black Rock (1,410 feet; 430 m), which is a great gift in the summer. I always carried lunch to eat on the highest point, where wind and sun both had full access to me. On Black Rock, I knew the fullest delight of a summer walk.

For more information, see the Hikers Region Map #12 (Black Rock Forest—Hudson Highlands West, Orange County, New York). This map is available at outdoor stores in New York or from Walking News, Inc., P.O. Box 352, New York, New York 10013.

Walks sometimes lead to unexpected finds.

NORTHWEST: Bear Trap Canyon

Another favorite of mine—this one a winter walk in Montana. Bear Trap Canyon was the first Wilderness designated by the Bureau of Land Management. The designation is the result of the Wilderness Act passed by Congress in 1964. *Wilderness*, with a capital W, is an official designation of land that protects it from development or anything mechanized. You cannot, for instance, use a chainsaw to cut apart a tree that has fallen over a path. Nor can you build a cabin or a road. You may walk in Wilderness, or ride a horse in it. Of course there is much wilderness in America that has not been designated as Wilderness.

This walk winds along the Madison River at the bottom of a narrow canyon the river has carved. The trail, which is basically level, with a few short, low rises, crosses open meadows, passes through some lovely rock and through river grasses and woods. And, always, the river is there, wide and almost calm, running in rapids, cresting white against rocks, grey in a storm, sparkling in sun. Above, to the east, high meadows and boulder fields rise up toward the rocky peaks of the Madison Range. To the west, the canyon walls descend in boulder fields, talus slopes, and steep rock. I almost always see an eagle overhead.

Fishermen are on the river year-round. Rafters float it spring through fall. Walkers use it in all seasons, although they are much rarer in winter (when, of course, most Montanans are off skiing). When I walked there on New Year's Day, the wind whipped down canyon and cross canyon with such force that the water seemed to move in constant opposition to itself—the current heading downstream; the rapids falling upstream in a white tumble of foam against the rocks; water spray gusting in low, rapid clouds across stream. It was as if I could *see* the wind.

Access to the canyon is only from the parking area reached by Norris Road (Route 84) at the canyon's north end. (River runners can put in at the south end, but there is no entry to the footpath from there.) The only way most walkers ever go the path's full distance is by camping overnight. Daywalkers simply walk whatever distance is comfortable, then turn back along the path to return.

The trail makes a good winter walk because it seems to have its own private climate and, although it does get a lot of wind, it is relatively snow free. Parts of it lying literally at the river's edge are sometimes icy, but these sections are short.

For more information, write Bear Trap Canyon, Butte District Office, Bureau of Land Management, P.O. Box 3388, Butte, Montana 59702. Or call 406-494-5059.

EARTH
WATCH

Because trails near metropolitan areas, like this one through Bear Trap Canyon, are heavily used, real care is needed in their continuing use. Walk lightly, leaving nothing behind but footsteps, taking nothing but memories and photographs. Sign the registration forms at the trailhead so that the BLM, which administers the Bear Trap Canyon Wilderness Area, can see the necessity for more walking trails. Urge them, and other federal agencies, to protect other wild areas. Get involved in volunteer trail-building programs so that there are alternative places to go for a walk. Walk trails in off-seasons, when use is way down. In 11 winters of walking in Bear Trap Canyon, I've never encountered another walker on a winter weekday.

SOUTHEAST: Corkscrew Swamp Sanctuary

There *is* a Florida apart from the tourist beaches. It is a unique place, without crowds, and provides a sense of what this land was before we covered so much of it with condominiums, roads, and shopping malls. In the southwestern corner of the state, slightly north and west of the Big Cypress National Preserve and Everglades National Park, is the National Audubon Society's Corkscrew Swamp Sanctuary. A short walk here—it's about a mile and three-quarters (2.8 km), most of it on an elevated boardwalk—takes you from sanctuary headquarters through a slice of the sanctuary's 11,000 acres (4,455 ha). You walk through pine forest that eases into waving grass and sedge, then into a stand of virgin bald cypress, the oldest trees in eastern North America. Epiphytes (air plants) cling to the trees, while ropelike roots of the strangler fig wind their way down the trunks. Ferns and wax myrtle are everywhere. So are birds. (This area, like most of Florida, is a birdwatcher's paradise. One of two major remaining rookeries of the wood stork is here.) Alligators sun themselves on floating logs.

There are bench areas, shelters, and an observation platform along the way. The guidebook you receive when you pay your admission gives you an immense amount of information about the exotic world through which you walk.

The sanctuary is open every day, May through November from 8 a.m. to 5 p.m. and, in winter, from 7 a.m. to 5 p.m. There is an admission fee of $6.50 for adults (or $5 for Audubon Society members) and $3 for students. To get there, take I-75 to the Naples Park exit (Exit 17), then drive 13 miles

20.8 km) east on Immokalee Road. For more information write to the Corkscrew Swamp Sanctuary, 375 Sanctuary Road, Naples, Florida 33964. Or call 813-657-3771.

© Courtesy of Corkscrew Swamp Sanctuary, Florida

The view along the Corkscrew Swamp Sanctuary's forested boardwalk.

SOUTHWEST: *Canyon de Chelly National Monument*

In the heart of Navajo country, Canyon de Chelly is a great, silent, ancient place in which you feel the immeasurable presence of time. The walls of the steep canyons that are all a part of the monument shelter the ruins of Anasazi cliff dwellings. There are over 700 ruin sites here, petroglyphs and cliff dwellings, representing both prehistoric Anasazi and historic Navajo times.

The only trail in the monument you can walk without a guide is the trail to White House Ruins, an easy trail that winds down over rounded red sandstone, coming, after the dark few feet of a tunnel, to the canyon floor. It is a glorious arrival. There is, literally, the light at the end of the tunnel, a grove of cottonwood, a deep blue sky. There is the river, the hogan of a Navajo family who farms the fertile land of the canyon floor, and, beyond

© Canyon de Chelley National Monument/Russ Finley

Canyon de Chelly's barren sandstone cliffs offer a stark contrast to the greenery of the canyon below.

the hogan, their sheep. You must stay on the trail here, however curious you may be. A walker is very much a visitor here.

It is a short walk along the canyon floor (the opposite direction from the hogan) to the ruins. The walk parallels the river, lined with cottonwoods. In autumn, the leaves ripple like flowing gold. A makeshift bridge crosses the river to bring you to the cliff on which the ruins stand. Ceilings and walls have decayed and fallen away so that you can see the ancient mud bricks defining the ruined rooms. In the field below the ruins, there are cholla and prickly pear cactus, a grove of willows and cottonwoods, a hot sun, and a cool breeze.

This is a walk that is almost entirely descent and climb, but the switchbacks are gentle ones and any time you stop to rest, you are rewarded with one more remarkable view. The entire round-trip is only about 2-1/2 miles (4 km). It is not a hard walk, but do carry water in this hot, dry climate.

For information, write the Superintendent, Canyon de Chelly National Monument, P.O. Box 588, Chinle, Arizona 86503. Or call 602-674-5500.

To find the special trails near you, or any of the other trails in your region, contact a local hiking club or conservationist organization, natural history museum or association, specialty outdoor shop, university outing club, or a National Audubon or Sierra Club chapter.

Canadian Trails

Just north of the U.S. border near Niagara Falls, the **Bruce Trail** begins at Niagara, Ontario. Following the Niagara Escarpment, with its grottos, waterfalls, caves, meadows, and forests north, it crosses rolling farmland, passes through towns and cities, abandoned dams, kilns, and mill houses to end 740 kilometers (460 miles) later on the spectacular cliffs of the Bruce Peninsula, a narrow arm of land dividing the waters of Georgian Bay from Lake Huron. Much of this trail can be done as day walks, with backroads and side trails making loops possible. For longer treks—whether overnight or 6 weeks—there are campsites and water sources the length of the trail, as well as commercial lodging a bit off the trail in towns along the way.

The northernmost part of the trail is the most glorious. The Bruce Peninsula is a land of limestone cliffs and caves, forested valleys lush with rare ferns, 39 varieties of wild orchids, and enough species of birds to satisfy almost anybody's life list. Bays and inlets, rocky beaches, and giant boulders line the waters of Georgian Bay. Topping off the whole experience of the region are the trails on Flowerpot Island, which lies just off the end of the peninsula. Accessible via water taxi from the town of Tobermory (which marks the end of the Bruce Trail), the island is a national park laced with trails leading to water-sculpted rock and caves in rugged limestone cliffs.

A guidebook to the Bruce Trail is available from the Bruce Trail Association, Box 857, Hamilton, Ontario L8N 3N9, Canada. Or call 905-529-6821. The guide costs $20 (Canadian) for nonmembers or $15 for

Colorful waters along the shoreline of Bruce Peninsula.

association members; it provides complete maps and trail information. A *Bed & Breakfast Guide*, also available from the association for $5, coordinates bed and breakfasts with the trail. (A bed and breakfast guide is also available free from the Ontario Tourist Office. It lists the same places, but it is a general guide and not coordinated with the trail.) Membership in the Bruce Trail Association costs $30 and entitles you to their quarterly news magazine as well as discounts on their publications and other merchandise. You may order the guidebook by phone and charge it to your Visa or Mastercard. You may also pay in American dollars, and the small difference in currency value gets donated to the Bruce Trail general fund, a worthy conservationist cause.

The Bruce Trail is one of eight long-distance hiking trails in Ontario, totaling more than 2,080 kilometers (1,300 miles). For addresses of the associations maintaining each, see the appendix. The eight are coordinated by Hike Ontario, 1220 Sheppard Avenue East, Willowdale, Ontario M2K

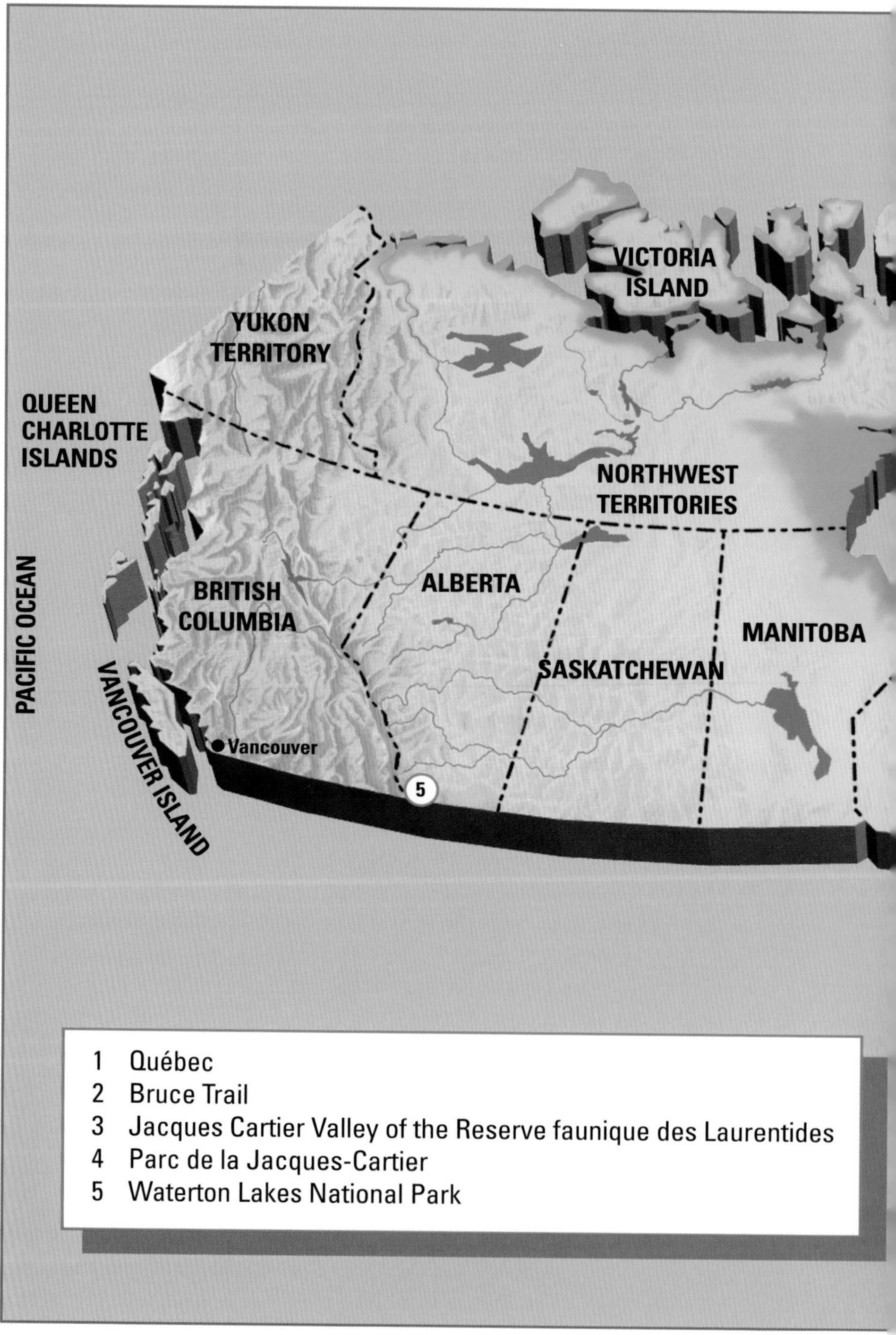

QUEEN CHARLOTTE ISLANDS

YUKON TERRITORY

VICTORIA ISLAND

NORTHWEST TERRITORIES

PACIFIC OCEAN

BRITISH COLUMBIA

ALBERTA

SASKATCHEWAN

MANITOBA

VANCOUVER ISLAND

●Vancouver

⑤

1 Québec
2 Bruce Trail
3 Jacques Cartier Valley of the Reserve faunique des Laurentides
4 Parc de la Jacques-Cartier
5 Waterton Lakes National Park

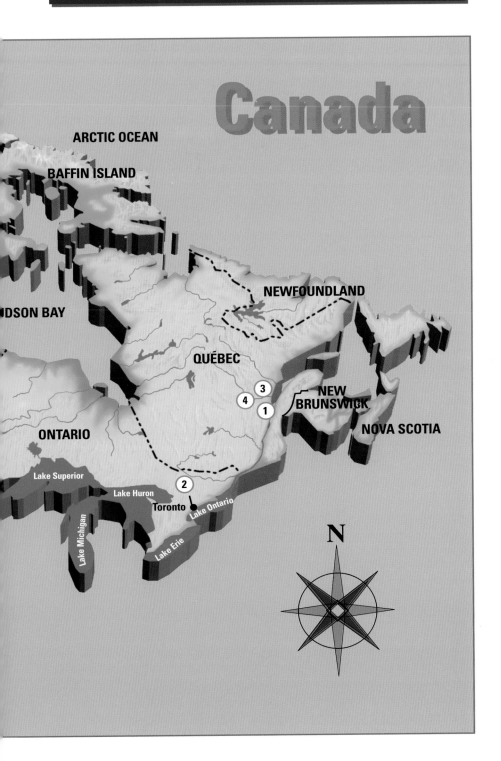

2X1, Canada. For information about Ontario in general, including hiking, canoeing, cycling, horseback riding, country inns, and anything else you'd like to know, call 800-668-2746.

In Québec, about an hour's drive north of the city of Québec, is the **Jacques Cartier Valley of the Reserve faunique des Laurentides**, a wildlife reserve that is a properly rugged, wild place. Its timbered mountains and glacier-scoured gorges are still inhabited by bear, moose, and otters. This is the Québec of Jacques Cartier, the 16th-century explorer who arrived in 1535 on commission by the King of France to explore the Saguenay and incidentally discovered the St. Lawrence. The area is laced with marked trails of varying length and difficulty, all branching off a dirt road that parallels the Jacques Cartier River. You can spend a week backpacking here, or a few hours walking on one of the trails. For more information, write to the Reserve faunique des Laurentides, 801 Chemin Saint Louis, Bureau 180, Québec, Québec G1S 1C1, Canada. Or call 418-686-1717.

South of the reserve and closer to town is the **Parc de la Jacques-Cartier**, one of Québec's 17 provincial parks. There are a good number of hiking trails here, too, that make for an easy day's walk. For more information, write Parc de la Jacques-Cartier, 9530 de la Faune, Charlesbourg, Québec G1G 5H9, Canada. Call 418-622-4444.

In Alberta, **Waterton Lakes National Park** (adjacent to Montana's Glacier National Park) is relatively small and extraordinarily beautiful. It is laced with one of the best (and most used) trail systems in the Canadian Rockies. The walk to Crypt Lake is a popular one in which access is via boat from the Waterton townsite to Hell Roaring dock. (Arrange with the boat operator to be picked up later.) The walk itself takes you past Hell Roaring Falls to end at the lovely alpine lake—after a climb of 701 meters (2,300 feet) in 8.8 kilometers (5-1/2 miles). Although this is a well-established and heavily used trail, a portion of it is fairly exposed, making it unsuitable for acrophobics. For more information on this and other park trails, write to the Superintendent, Waterton Lakes National Park, Waterton Park, Alberta T0K 2M0, Canada. Call 403-859-2224.

British Pathways

Of all the places on earth to go for a walk, none seems as purely romantic as England. Maybe it's the aura of 19th-century English novels. Maybe it's the high moors, the mist, the intense green of deep forest, the old villages nestling in a rolling countryside. (Where, of course, all the 19th-century English novels take place.) In any case, it seems to me the ultimate place to go for a walk. Indeed, it has more public footpaths than any nation on earth. In England and Wales alone, the network is 192,000 kilometers (120,000 miles) long. There is no place in the country that does not offer the possibility of a good walk. In Scotland, you may walk anywhere.

Britain courts its walkers. The British Tourist Authority publishes a marvelous brochure, *Britain for Walkers*, that presents all the National Trails in England and Wales, long-distance routes in Scotland, and a selection of regional routes across Britain. It includes sample itineraries designed to give you an idea of the kinds of walks possible and provides a list of guidebooks and maps. The brochure is actually a large, foldout map that shows you where all the trails are so you can pick your walk based on where in England you'd like to be. For any true walker, this map is indispensable. (The British Tourist Authority is also careful to point out that the brochure is made from the woodpulp of managed forests and for every tree cut down, at least one tree is planted.)

The Tourist Authority will also send you the brochures of a number of companies that run guided walks through England, Scotland, Wales, and Ireland, as well as one company that will map out unescorted walking tours in which they arrange everything, including your baggage transfers.

Close to London, and reached at various intervals by train and bus routes, the Surrey end of the **North Downs Way** (a 245-kilometer, or 153-mile, route across rolling farmland, over wooded and open hillsides, across heath and valley, and through charming villages) is part of a greenbelt preservation. Part of it follows the ancient Pilgrim's Way, the route followed by medieval travelers from Winchester to Canterbury (the North Downs Way does not actually go to Canterbury, but a northern alternative route does). Walking the entire North Downs Way gives you an extraordinary sense of this country, but doing bits and pieces of it is also satisfying. You can find lodging in the towns along the way—which is, incidentally, a good deal cheaper than staying in London.

There is a complete description of this route in a guidebook called *Walker's Britain*, which, along with its companion, *Walker's Britain 2*, describes over 400 walks. These are the most complete guidebooks to *anywhere* I've ever seen, providing maps, detailed information about the walks themselves, the countryside, the villages, and the historic sites along the way. The second volume includes descriptions of canal towpath and abandoned railway walks. The first volume provides a rundown on Britain's long-distance paths, including the **Pennine Way**, which runs 410 kilometers (256 miles) from the Peak of Derbyshire to the Scottish Border. The first of England's long-distance paths, the Pennine Way now counts as second longest, after the 828-kilometer (518-mile) South West Peninsula Coast Path. The Pennine Way, which passes through the heart of Bronte country, crosses some of the roughest and most remote areas of England. In its entirety, it is a strenuous, challenging walk, although parts of it lie within easy reach of densely populated areas.

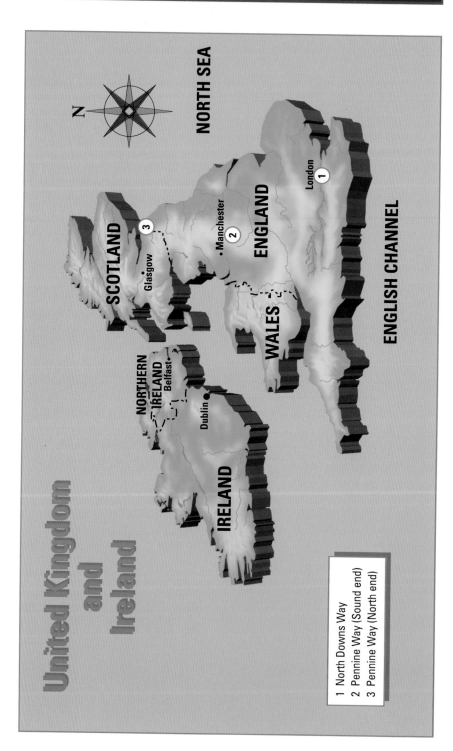

United Kingdom
and
Ireland

NORTH SEA

SCOTLAND

Glasgow

ENGLAND

Manchester

London

WALES

ENGLISH CHANNEL

NORTHERN
IRELAND

Belfast

Dublin

IRELAND

N

1 North Downs Way
2 Pennine Way (Sound end)
3 Pennine Way (North end)

Two Pennine Way guidebooks (north and south) are a part of the official guides to National Trails in England and Wales published in conjunction with the Countryside Commission and Ordinance Survey. (You'll use Ordinance Survey maps no matter where you choose to walk in Britain.) These official guides, and a slew of others, are easily available in Britain. The British Travel Centre at 12 Regent Street, Piccadilly Circus, London SW1Y 4PQ, is open 7 days a week and can give you information and guidebooks for the whole of Britain.

The *Walker's Britain* books are available at Powell's Travel Store (a bookstore devoted solely to travel books) at 701 S.W. 6th Street, Portland, Oregon 97204. Call 503-228-1108. Powell's is the place to contact for walking guides to anywhere in the world, for both cities and backcountry. Tell them the region that interests you, and they'll tell you what books they have. If they don't have it, you will probably only be able to get it at the place itself.

For the address of the British Tourist Authority and the tourist offices of the other countries mentioned here, from whom you can get more specific information about walking, please see the appendix. Among the questions you must ask is whether or not you need a visa.

Wandering Western Europe

I've spent a good deal of my life walking in the Alps—on paths that have been walked for centuries by shepherds and farmers, artists, writers, romantics (who often carried out scientific studies because, until the mid-19th century, walking in the mountains purely for pleasure was considered suspect), and other assorted travelers. The paths, leading into the inner recesses of the mountains, across high meadows and through alpine villages, serve Sunday strollers as well as serious hikers and climbers on their way to the peaks.

These old (but well-marked and well-tended by national alpine clubs) paths invite the walker into personal journeys. The cable cars and mountain railways that transport walkers into the good paths of the high country, allowing one to walk miles at high altitude, make these paths accessible to everyone. Except for the vagaries of mountain weather (to which you must pay strict attention) even the most dramatic walks become relatively easy.

You walk through green valleys and high meadows, over windswept rocky passes, along the sides of jagged, grey mountains, through forests and across barren moonscapes, to come, each day, to a mountain hut. Tired, thirsty, hungry, you can eat and drink and sleep and tomorrow go on again.

European Destinations

1 Mont Blanc, France

2 Bernese Oberland,
  Switzerland

3 Mount Olympus, Greece

4 Allgäuer Alps
  (near Oberstdorf), Germany

5 Dolomite Alps, Italy

6 Scharnitz, Austria

In Europe, a vast system of refuges (huts) of varying degrees of primitiveness offers shelter and a place to sleep, as well as food that may vary from a bowl of soup to a full course dinner complete with wine. Although there are some places where you should carry a sleeping bag (notably, Sweden), in general one need not. Prepared food and bedding are all part of this system that allows ordinary walkers the taste of high adventure. Whether you want to make a short walk, a day's walk, or a walk of days, there are trails for every level of walker—challenging paths and easy ones. The easy ones are full of places where lazy adults, small children, and dogs can lie in lovely meadows while the more ambitious can take off to climb some peak, or walk a more challenging route, and return a few hours later to go on to the hut.

Some particularly lovely places to walk in Europe include the Mont Blanc region near Chamonix in France; in the Bernese Oberland, from Kandersteg to Meiringen, Switzerland; up Mount Olympus in Greece; through the Allgäuer Alps near the town of Oberstdorf, Germany; and in the Italian Dolomites from Santa Cristina to the Marmolada. Although I have walked extensively in France, Switzerland, and Italy, I tend to use Austria (perhaps because I lived there) as the example of what mountain life is like. Austria has lovely, gentle trails leading from hut to hut. It also has wild, high arêtes and summits, glittering, vast, and lonely glaciers, and a soul to match its mountains—impassive and passionate at once, restrained, and practical yet extravagant. The high mountains are stern and cold, the lower ones warmly beckoning with their lush, green meadows and myriad wildflowers. Despite an enormously cosmopolitan history, the mountain people are the heart of the country. The cities are there, with their music and culture and old sophistication, retaining still the rococo trappings of empire, but nothing masks the land itself.

A WANDERING SONG

Ist das nicht ein wunderbares Leben
frei wie Zigeuner wir sind

This is a song people sing in the German-speaking huts. "As free as gypsies," it says. The sentiment is perhaps a bit dated, but I cling to it as I cling to the freedom of being a vagabond. It goes on ". . . drawn here and there as the wind, sometimes staying where the world is especially beautiful . . . Is that not a wondrous life?"

Walking in the mountains *is* wondrous. Free and unfettered, it erases the memories of a settled life and removes the need for a future. The mountains are eternal. Life is in the moment, and it is enough.

There is a special attitude in Austria toward the mountains and all who go into them. And because Austria has no Jungfrau, no Mont Blanc, the people who come to the mountains come not to ogle but to walk. Even day hikers here are people who come often. They know what the mountains are about and are at home in them. One of my favorite walks here is a relaxed 3-day trip beginning at the town of **Scharnitz** (a short train ride from Innsbruck). The first day is the hardest, with a 5-hour walk that climbs more than 792 meters (2,600 feet) (mostly in the last stretch) as you approach the first hut, the Karwendelhaus, a large, handsome hut built at the very edge of the mountain. On my first walk here, I arrived in a cold rainstorm but found a warm place by the stove in the beautiful old wooden common room for dinner.

I was assigned a bed in a bunk in a small dormitory room and, when it was time, I was glad to get into it. I had, however, not been in it very long when a German man came into the room, saw me in the bunk and, blushing, excused himself while backing out of the room. "Oh, I'm sorry," he said, "I'm in the wrong room. I'm so sorry. I thought it was this room. In fact, there are my things over there on that bunk, but it must be the wrong room." "This is the right room," I said to him. "Everybody sleeps together. In the same room." "Oh," he said, "I've never stayed overnight before."

From the Karwendelhaus, the path descends slightly to the Kleiner Ahornboden, a flat, lush, green meadow that gets its name from the maple (*Ahorn*) trees that grow there. The meadow is like a garden, an Elizabethan lawn, a meeting ground for magical creatures, doubly enchanting in the midst of all the rock, steep meadowland, and towering wild mountains surrounding it. I sat awhile under a maple tree (I usually sit under any beautiful tree in any beautiful spot I come to. I find taking the time to sit a very important part of walking. Sometimes it is time to sort out the things I think as I walk; sometimes it is time to dream; sometimes it is time for lunch; sometimes it is time simply to sit beneath the tree) before getting underway again and crossing a dried-up river bed.

Climbing up out of the Kleiner Ahornboden, I came to a meadow where farmers come with their stock for the summer. A few farmers waved to me, and I stopped to rest on the porch on one of their huts. The door was open so that inside I could see a rough table and bench, some blackened pots on the wall, and a corner fireplace. I smelled potatoes roasting in the fireplace. The room opened onto another room behind it, earth-floored, lined with shelves holding huge wheels of aging cheese. Two vats on the floor contained the partially processed cheese. Turning away from the hut, I watched a pig walk up to the water trough and jump in. He waded the length of the trough, then climbed out.

The farmers who summer up here with their cattle and pigs live the rest of the year in the Eng Valley, the next valley on this walk. I climbed the last steep meadow to the next hut, the Falkenhutte, a 3-hour walk from the

© Austrian Tourist Office

The Alps offer trails for every level of walker.

Karwendelhaus. There were a few people there on day walks up from the Eng Valley for lunch.

The following day I walked 2 hours down to the Eng Valley, a walk easy enough to leave me time to dawdle in a pretty, high meadow opposite a massive rock wall. I had walked beneath the wall earlier on my way to this meadow, hearing along the way the rumble of falling stones. As I sat in the meadow, I heard a roar like thunder, and, suddenly, an avalanche of stones cascaded down the wall in a grey-brown cloud. The cloud rolled, roaring down the mountain, growing larger and larger as it rolled, until it covered the path I had walked. The roaring ended, but the cloud held an echo of the falling rocks, until, silent, it began to rise. Then, as if the cascade had never happened, the path was clear and the mountains quiet.

I descended into the little farming village at the end of the Eng Valley and stopped for lunch at a restaurant there. Sitting at a table outside in the sun, I felt no need to rush. Afterward, I walked on (and mostly up) another 2 hours through meadows filled with wildflowers to the next hut, the Lamsenjochhutte. (I could also have stayed in the Eng, as I had in the past. If you decide to stay, ask about accommodations at the restaurant or at the hotel at the farther end of the village.)

The Lamsenjochhutte nestles in a spectacular world of high mountains. It seems almost impossible, when you look at a photo of it, that you could ever get there just by walking. But, like so much here, it truly is just a walk. For walkers traveling with a climber, though, there are plenty of things here (and along this entire route) to climb, whether one is a technical climber or a scrambler.

The next morning, I walked down, out of this world of rock, into woods, through the Wolfsklamm, a ravine whose paths weave around waterfalls, and over the stream that cuts the ravine. I continued down the path past neat farms and on into the town of Schwaz with its pretty Tyrolian houses. Geraniums and roses grow everywhere. From Schwaz, I took the train back to Innsbruck.

It was a lovely walk and typical of a walk in the Alps. I've done it many times, in all kinds of weather and conditions. Each time seems entirely different so that what I have learned from it (and from those other walks I've done more than once) is that you could probably spend your lifetime in one place, and each time you walked there, something new would happen. Being able to travel to go for a walk is marvelous, but I think that what is *new* is everywhere.

Guided hut-to-hut walks in Austria (and other countries) are superbly conducted by the Alpinschule Innsbruck, In der Stille 1, 6161 Natters, Austria. Call 0512/54 60 00. Contact them for their catalog. They also run free day walks from Innsbruck and Igls. Inquire at the Tourist Office.

Tramping Down Under

NEW ZEALAND

The ideal thing about New Zealand, aside from being spectacular, is that, if you live in North America, you can walk all spring, summer, and fall in (relatively) good weather at home, then spend winter having summer in New Zealand. A lot of people do it—so many that some of the more popular routes are not only crowded but bear heavy regulations in order to keep the experience as pristine as possible for those who walk there.

New Zealand, like Europe, has a hut system, but their huts are more primitive, requiring you to carry a sleeping bag to overnight in them and to

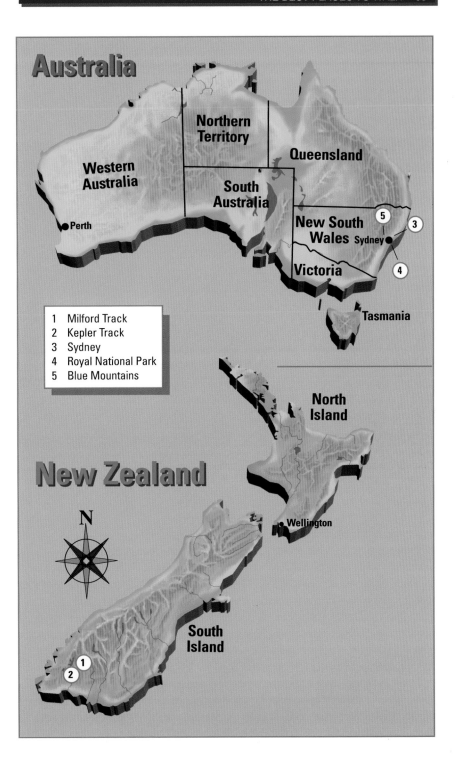

Australia

Northern Territory

Western Australia

Queensland

•Perth

South Australia

New South Wales Sydney•

5

3

Victoria

4

Tasmania

1 Milford Track
2 Kepler Track
3 Sydney
4 Royal National Park
5 Blue Mountains

New Zealand

North Island

N

•Wellington

South Island

1

2

Dense vegetation along New Zealand's Routebourn Track.

carry and cook your own food. The huts vary in size from one-room shacks with not much besides a fireplace, table, and canvas mattress to 40-bunk buildings with separate kitchens and flush toilets. The fees for huts vary. Tickets for them, or Great Walks Passes (if you mean to spend considerable time on New Zealand's walking tracks), should be purchased in advance. They are available from the Department of Conservation offices or park visitor centers. For more information about walking in all of New Zealand's Parks and Reserves, contact the Department of Conservation, Te Papa Atawhai, P.O. Box 10410, Wellington, New Zealand.

One day, a national walkway will run from one end of New Zealand to the other. The walkway concept began as a way of providing access for short family walks into the countryside, easily accessible from urban areas. In fact, the walkways built around the country vary considerably in difficulty and terrain, with many of them suitable only for experienced backcountry hikers. But because the New Zealand Walkways Commission has set up a system of track classifications that rates all of them, you can easily avoid getting off on the wrong one. The easiest rating is a *walk*—a path suitable for the average family. Next is a *track*—a well-defined walking track suitable for people of good to average physical fitness. Most difficult is a *route*—a lightly marked trail meant for well-equipped, experienced hikers.

Of the walkways rated *easy*, the most popular is the **Milford Track**, a 4-day walk from Glade Wharf to Milford Sound in Fiordland National Park on the South Island. The Milford Track is probably the first name anybody thinks of when New Zealand is mentioned. Because of the heavy summer (mid-December to January) traffic on this track, there are numerous regulations regarding its use, including that you may walk only in the direction from Glade Wharf to Milford Sound in summer and must walk it in 3 nights and 4 days or less, whether the weather turns bad or not. (The strict regulations make the track appear less crowded than it actually is.) This is a walk you must book in advance, which you can do by writing the Tourist Hotel Corporation, P.O. Box 185, Te Anau, New Zealand. There are other routes in the park as well. The **Kepler Track** is especially good for half-day and day walks.

If you're planning a trip down under, you would do well to get hold of a thorough guidebook to walking in New Zealand called *Tramping in New Zealand* by Jim DuFresne; it's available at American bookstores or from Lonely Planet, Embarcadero West, 155 Filbert Street, Oakland, California 94607. Forty tracks are described in the book, and you should find some that suit your walking needs. The book gives you all the information you need for any walking trip in New Zealand, including how to make arrangements for your trip.

AUSTRALIA

Aside from the magnificence of its scenery and the oddity—for most other English speakers—of its language, Australia, isolated as an island for so long, has a completely separate fauna and flora. Whereas New Zealand looks much like the mountain country of the western United States and Canada and the Alps and feels somehow familiar to Americans, Australia is completely foreign. The plants, for instance, have been there so long that they've all developed enormous self-protection with things that poke, stick, prick, and jab. The animals exist nowhere else. Kangaroos, wombats, Tasmanian devils, koalas, platypuses, echidnas, dingoes, kookaburras, emus, casowaries . . . the list goes on. Of course, there are also crocodiles, spiders, and sand flies, but in the face of all the exotic animals, I can't help but find these creatures less interesting, if more of a nuisance.

Sydney, Australia's largest city, in New South Wales, Australia's oldest state, is a good place for walkers. Ringed by national parks, there is an enormous variety of what the Australians call "bushwalking" in every direction from town, and there is easy public transportation to much of it. Sydney's location, originally chosen because it offered a safe deepwater harbor and a freshwater stream, is the sort of location where, in most of the world, the natural scenery gave rapid way to farms, suburbs, and other development. Fortunately for nature, the country around Sydney is too wild for settlement, too deeply cut by river gorges, too filled with formidable cliffs, boulders, bare rock, and sandy, infertile soil to have been of use to settlers. Across the world, land deemed worthless by pioneers has often become the sole surviving natural habitat. In recent years more and more of this land has been officially protected for the special qualities that naturally protected it in the first place.

Royal National Park, the second oldest national park in the world (after Yellowstone), was established in 1879. It lies at the southern edge of the city. Regular public transportation provides access to each end of the park, and there is easy walking along its gorgeous coastline. (You can make a 2-day walk here and go from one end of the park to the other, but you have to camp to do this.)

West of town (and also accessible by public transportation) are the **Blue Mountains**. Their name comes from the blue mist that hangs over them much of the time and the sense of blue that comes from a forest composed almost entirely of the tall, slender blue gum tree. The absence of green is actually startling here. There is a muted grey-green that hints at some *memory* of green. This is a world made of all the tints and shadows of blue. You walk in this color's infinite moods.

A raised, fairly flat sandstone plateau deeply cut by water, the Blue Mountains are mainly exposed, high, vertical cliffs. Waterfalls are everywhere. Vegetation is thick. There are some steep ups and downs here, but you can make short walks that are not difficult.

The National Parks Authority has several brochures about the Blue Mountains National Park. These are available by writing to National Parks & Wildlife Service, P.O. Box 43, Blackheath, Australia 2785.

The most complete guide to walking in Australia available in the U.S. is Lonely Planet's *Bushwalking in Australia* by John and Monica Chapman, but the walks they describe take at least 2 days, and you must be equipped to camp to do them. (They are, however, rated from easy to hard, so if you're prepared to camp and decide to do any of them, at least you know what you're getting into.) For those interested in shorter walks, *Walks in the Blue Mountains* by Neil Paton covers that region well. Another useful book for day walkers is *100 Walks in New South Wales* by Tyrone Thomas. This one describes walks throughout the state. Both books should be available in outdoor (bushwalking) shops in Sydney, if you can't find them at Powell's in Portland.

One of the nicest things about the Lonely Planet books is that they describe every other guidebook to the region. Even if you never intend to follow the Lonely Planet treks, the books are valuable for all the information they present. They also adhere to a travel philosophy that I think is useful for any walker (actually, useful for anyone who happens to be alive): "Don't worry about whether your trip will work out. Just go!"

6

PURSUING WALKING FURTHER

Once you've become a con-
firmed walker, you may want to expand the varieties of walks you make.
There are a huge array of activities from which to choose. Trail hiking,
which is essentially what I've been talking about in the preceding travel
section, is probably the most obvious extension. Hiking can be more related
to jogging or to walking, depending on the kind of hiking you do. A gentle
stroll down a woodland path is a walk. A vigorous climb up a steep 6,000-
foot (1,829-m) mountain, with or without a pack, is a hike, a workout akin
to jogging. Any pitch increases the work you and your heart have to do, yet
a walk such as the walk I described down into, and then up out of, Canyon

de Chelly is really not a hard walk. Unless you have a physical condition that prevents you from climbing anything, don't be put off by *all* trails requiring a climb. It's perfectly fine to walk slowly.

Backcountry and Adventure Walking

For people who enjoy walking on backcountry trails, backpacking is a logical step. Here, by carrying all your equipment on your back—sleeping bag, tent, cooking equipment, food, and clothes—you can extend your walk to a matter of days. Self-sufficient, you sleep in the same outdoors where you walk. Backpacking allows you to go deeper into the territory, to experience it farther and farther from roads, to travel the many long trails like the Appalachian Trail from Maine to Georgia or the Pacific Crest Trail from Canada to Mexico.

© F-Stock/John Laptad

Hiking backcountry trails is a great way to stay in shape and see some astonishing scenery close-up.

WALKING TIP   For those who like the walk and the camping, but not the carrying, llamas make wonderful companions. They walk at your pace and carry all the gear. There are llama outfitters throughout the country. If you are considering getting a llama of your own, you must get at least two. They get too lonely alone and responsible breeders won't sell you just one.

If you go trekking in the Himalayas, you can hire Sherpas to carry the heavy stuff. Along the long trails in other parts of the world—the Pennine Way in England, the various long trails of Europe—there are villages or mountain refuges where you can overnight. (The Pennine Way has a few long stretches where you should have a tent. Or you might just decide to do other stretches of the trail.) For the most part, though, all you need to carry is a daypack with your clothes and toiletries, then find food and shelter in the huts. If you tramp through New Zealand or, in some areas of Australia, you need to carry a sleeping bag and food, but the huts allow you to forego the tent and stove.

Hiking, outdoor, and conservation clubs all over the country sponsor group outings, day hikes or backpacks, for those who prefer to go with a group. As you become more comfortable in wild settings, you may opt out of groups, deciding to go with one or two other people to improve your chances of seeing and hearing wildlife, or to experience a greater sense of the solitude for which so many of us go into wild country. If you'd like someone else to do the organizing, commercial outfits sponsor treks in all the exotic, challenging, magnificent places of the Earth. Some of these outfits are local operations specializing in their own vicinity, and you might decide on one of their treks once you get to where you're going. Others, like Overseas Adventure Travel, based in Cambridge, Massachusetts, or Progressive Travels, based in Washington state, operate internationally. Among their great variety of trips, Overseas Adventure Travel includes family trips to Costa Rica, the Galapagos, and the Canadian Rockies. These trips are not entirely walking, but they include walking and make for wonderful trips with children. Their adult trips—to the Himalayas, Asia, Africa, the Mediterranean, and the Americas—which often include a good deal more walking, are also extraordinary. For information, write to Overseas Adventure Travel, 349 Broadway, Cambridge, Massachusetts 02139. Or call 800-221-0814.

Progressive Travels specializes in walking and bicycling tours in France and Washington state (with a bit of Kenya thrown in). Walks average four to five hours (at your own pace) with good food and lodging ranging from country inns to castles awaiting you at the end. Your luggage is transported to your lodging, so you need carry no more than a daypack. For more information call 800-245-2229.

Organizations such as the Sierra Club and the Appalachian Mountain Club also run walking trips for various levels of walkers. See the appendix for addresses.

Speedwalking and Racewalking

Speedwalking is less about walking at specific speeds than about walking in a style that increases your forward velocity. Your arms pump close to your sides and your feet, having increased the strides you make per minute (from the usual 60 strides per minute up to 65 or 80), land in an almost straight line. Your posture is erect, with perhaps the slightest lean forward from the ankles.

Racewalking is similar to speedwalking, but there is a technical difference: Your knee must be straight when it is directly under the body and over your foot. It is this straightening of the knee that sends the hip swinging out and gives racewalkers the rather odd look they have in motion. I say "odd," but in fact there is a floating quality to the motion and the more expert you become at it, the more you will feel as if you're floating. If racewalking interests you, you might do well to attend a clinic in your area so that you have an expert on hand to make corrections before you get into wrong habits. There are racewalking clubs almost everywhere. For a directory of them, send a self-addressed stamped envelope to Bob Carlson, 2261 Glencoe Street, Denver, Colorado 80207. Mr. Carlson, whose Front Range Walkers has 430 members, calls racewalking the "technique that uses the biomechanics of the body to the utmost so you can walk efficiently, so you can go fast."

Watching Birds

Bird-watching usually requires that you walk at least a short distance to get away from traffic and other disturbances, that you do it very early in the morning, and that you spend considerable time standing around, or sitting quietly, binoculars or spotting scope in hand, waiting to see which birds are present. Bird-watching is a mesmerizing and rewarding activity, but it involves walking as a means rather than as a goal. There are times when more strenuous walks are required, such as those that get you into high country to watch fairly closely the annual migrations of hawks. *Walking Magazine* lists the annual Audubon Society Christmas Bird Count in its Events Column and, indeed, finding as many birds as you can in 24 hours does require some real moving. Check with your local Audubon Society or natural history museum for birding tours in other places, both nationally and internationally.

© Unicorn/Dick Keen

You may find that, for you, walking is definitely for the birds.

Orienteering

In orienteering, you use a map and compass to navigate from point to point in the landscape as quickly and efficiently as possible. The number of miles covered and the difficulty of the terrain can be decided according to the skill of the participants. As they go from point to point, orienteers, continually forced to make navigational decisions, learn to read the landscape, becoming fully able to assess and understand it.

The important equipment for orienteering are map and compass, and the prime job for the orienteer, beginner or not, is to know where he or she is on the map at all times. Orienteering can be a competitive sport, but its essence is that it is a personal skill, like walking itself, owing nothing to outside help. There are about 3,000 active competitive orienteers in the U.S., but tens of thousands use orienteering for other purposes, including noncompetitive recreation.

Orienteering is not complicated, but the words describing it are. The easiest way to learn is through an orienteering club, by doing. Clubs throughout the country hold meets for all levels of participants, beginners to experts. Even if you're not interested in anything competitive, you can still benefit from their information about local courses and maps. A list of clubs is available from Silva Orienteering Service USA, P.O. Box 1604, Binghamton, New York 13902.

CONSUMER TIP Simple compasses are as good as expensive ones for anyone but professional orienteers. You can buy good Silva compasses for $10 to $13. The best maps to use, aside from those made especially for orienteering meets, are USGS topographical maps, 7-1/2 minute series, with a scale of 1:24,000.

President's Certificate

For some people, keeping a log of walks provides an incentive to continue, even on the days when a walk is the last thing you feel like doing. While your own body provides the *real* log, a visible and sensual record of the fact that you have been walking, sometimes it's also encouraging to refer to a written log. Seeing how much you've done is a goad to doing more. Beyond the

Orienteering is a great way to hone your map-reading skills for backcountry hiking.

record keeping, however, a log can qualify you for the Presidential Sports Award. To qualify, you must walk a minimum of 125 miles. Each walk must be continuous, without pauses for rest, and you must walk at a pace of a mile in 15 minutes—that is, 4 miles per hour. No more than 2-1/2 miles a day may be credited to your total.

For those who have received this initial award, there are also racewalking and endurance walking awards. To qualify for the racewalking award, you must racewalk a minimum of 200 miles. Each walk must be continuous for at least 3 miles and no more than 5 miles on any one day can be counted toward the total. The miles must be spread over at least 40 outings. Your average walking time must be 12 minutes a mile or less. You must follow the basic rules of racewalking and participate in at least three judged events.

For the endurance walking award, you must walk a minimum of 225 miles. Your walks must be continuous for at least 5 miles, with no more than one 10-mile or 15-mile walk credited each week. During a 4-month period, at least five of your walks must be 10 miles long, and at least one must be 15 miles long. You must include four 1-hour walks a week.

Presidential Sports Award Walking Logs are available from the Superintendent of Documents, U.S. Government Printing Office, P.O. Box 371954, Pittsburgh, Pennsylvania 15250. Ask for *Walking for Exercise and Pleasure*, stock # 017-001-00447-2 and enclose a check for $1. Or, if you join the *Prevention* magazine walking club, use the log they provide you. Your completed log, along with a check for $6 (payable to AAU/Presidential Sports Award), should be sent to the Presidential Sports Award, AAU House, P.O. Box 68297, Indianapolis, Indiana 46268.

A Passion for Walking

I began serious walking when my father took me for my first hike when I was two. For me, walking led to hiking mountains and to backpacking, although I walk *everywhere*. Nothing pleases me more than to walk hours in New York or Chicago or Paris or Florence. I relish walks on city streets or in city parks. When I travel by car with my dog, we seek out parks in the towns through which we pass, or natural preserves at the towns' edges. In this way I've come upon wonderful trails all across America. Towns I might have rushed through, noticing nothing but the motel where I spent the night, I've left instead with a feeling for their uniqueness. In fact, since my dog and I began traveling together, I often aim for a town because my AAA book says there is a nice park near or in it.

I've led groups of hikers on backpacks and on day hikes throughout the Northeast and in the Northern Rocky Mountains, and I have taken an

Walking furthers your connections to your surroundings and to those you choose to take along.

occasional friend with me on a walk in the Alps. But I love to walk alone as well. I love the intimacy with the earth that walking alone gives me. When you walk alone, there is nothing but you and the land. There is no distraction from its steepness or its flatness, its contours, its flowers, grasses, trees, and rocks, its winds, its sun, clouds, and storms, its ease, and its challenges. You enter into the land in the fullest possible way.

Yet, to share all of this with someone who cares about it as you do, who may never have experienced it before and now, because of you, feels its grandeur and its simplicity, or who can bring you further into it than you have ever been, and, consequently, further into your own feelings about your connection to the earth and your strength in that connection—all of these are also ways of entering into the land in the fullest possible way.

Going for a walk is about entering into the vitality of the city, the calm of the park, the wonder of the nature preserve, and the wildness of mountain, seashore, badlands, and forest. Walking is a responsible act. You take responsibility for your presence in a place. You are not carried mindlessly along. Whether you walk for the adventure, the exercise, the opportunity to think, the chance to look at the scenery, or to be with someone, doesn't matter. What matters is that you are taking action in a world where real action is rare. This may lead some people to find you odd, but what you are is free. What you are is a walker.

APPENDIX

FOR MORE INFORMATION

National Tourist Offices

First, a note about contacting these offices. None of them but the Canadian and the Austrian offices is easy to reach by phone. They all have complicated systems that make it very hard to reach an actual person, so it might take you less time to send a note requesting information. Most of these offices provide fairly general information. For more details, you'll have to write or visit another office in the region where you plan to walk. This is easy to do (unless you arrive on a weekend) and a good idea because the local people know their walking trails and will have good suggestions for you regarding routes, lodging, weather, and so on. If you plan to write to an office, allow several weeks for mail to go back and forth.

Austrian National Tourist Office
Travel Information Center
P.O. Box 1142
New York, NY 10108-1142
212-944-6880

Ask for their brochure, *Hiking and Backpacking in Austria*. They will also send you information about the Austrian Alpine Club

(Oesterreichischer Alpenverein). Membership ($55 for one adult, $40 for a spouse, $15 for ages 6 through 18) cuts your mountain hut lodging costs in half and gets you discounts on mountain transportation as well.

Australian Tourist Commission
100 Park Avenue, 25th floor
New York, NY 10017
212-687-6300

or

2121 Avenue of the Stars, Suite 1200
Los Angeles, CA 90067
310-552-1988

> *Bushwalking in Australia* lists Tourist Offices in Australia, where you might get the most complete information. The guidebook also lists companies that run guided walking tours.

British Tourist Authority
551 Fifth Avenue, Suite 701
New York, NY 10016-0799
212-986-2266

> Ask for their brochure *Britain for Walkers,* which includes a foldout map of Britain and the major walking paths. Also request their brochures on walking tours.

Ontario Travel
Queen's Park
Toronto, Ontario
Canada M7A 2R9
800-668-2746

> For information about Ontario's eight long-distance trails, including maps, contact these addresses:
>
> Avon Trail, Box 20018, Stratford, Ontario, Canada N5A 7V3. 62 miles (99 km).
>
> Bruce Trail Association, Box 857, Hamilton, Ontario, Canada L8N 3N9. 460 miles (736 km).
>
> Ganaraska Trail Association, 12 King Street, Box 19 Orillia, Ontario, Canada L3V 1R1. 124 miles (198 km).
>
> Grand Valley Trails Association, Box 1233, Kitchener, Ontario, Canada N2G 4G8. 77 miles (123 km).
>
> Guelph Trail Club, Box 1, Guelph, Ontario, Canada N1H 6J6. 40 miles (64 km).

Maitland Trail Association, P.O. Box 443, Goderich, Ontario, Canada N7A 4C7. About 18 miles (29 km).

Rideau Trail Association, Box 15, Kingston, Ontario, Canada K7L 4V6. 250 miles (400 km).

Thames Valley Trail Association, c/o Grovenor Lodge, 1017 Weston Road, London, Ontario, Canada N6G 1G5. 37 miles (59 km).

Greater Québec Area Tourism and Convention Bureau
399 rue Saint-Joseph est
Québec, Québec
Canada G1K 8E2
800-363-7777

> For information about walking in the city of Québec, contact the Québec Tourism Office, 399 Saint Joseph East, Québec, Québec, Canada G1K 8E2. 418-522-3511.

Alberta Chamber of Commerce
2105 Toronto Dominion Tower
Edmonton Center
Edmonton, Alberta, Canada T5J 2Z1
403-425-4180

British Columbia Chamber of Commerce
1607 700 West Pender Street
Vancouver, British Columbia, Canada V6C 1G8
604-683-0700

> I haven't mentioned walks in British Columbia, but this is gorgeous country and both Vancouver and Victoria are interesting cities.

French Government Tourist Office
610 Fifth Avenue
New York, NY 10020
212-757-1125

Italian Government Tourist Office
For people living in the eastern half of the U.S.:
630 5th Avenue
New York, NY 10111.
212-245-4822

For people living in the western half of the U.S.:
360 Post St.
San Francisco, CA 94108
415-392-6206

New Zealand Tourism Board
501 Santa Monica Boulevard, Suite 300
Santa Monica, CA 90401
Attn: Information Section
800-388-5494 or 310-395-7480

Ask for their brochures *Explore New Zealand*, which will give you further addresses to contact in New Zealand, and *Trek New Zealand*, which will give you information about guided tours on five popular tracks.

Swiss National Tourist Office
608 5th Avenue
New York, NY 10020
212-757-5944

or

150 North Michigan Avenue, Suite 2930
Chicago, Illinois 60601
312-630-5840

or

222 North Sepulveda Boulevard, Suite 1570
El Segundo, CA 90245
310-335-5980

For Information About Clubs Sponsoring Trips for Walkers

Some of these groups are national, some regional. Those that are national have regional chapters.

New York–New Jersey Trail Conference, Inc.
232 Madison Ave., Suite 401
New York, NY 10016
212-685-9699

This organization can provide information about trails in the New York–New Jersey region.

Sierra Club
730 Polk Street
San Francisco, CA 94109
415-776-2211

The Sierra Club can provide you information about local chapters, which exist all over the U.S.

Appalachian Mountain Club
5 Joy Street
Boston, MA 02108
607-523-0636

This club can provide you with information about local chapters throughout the east, as well as information about the hut system they maintain in New Hampshire's White Mountains.

American Volkssport Association
1001 Pat Booker Road, Suite 101
Universal City, TX 78148

Volkssporting, translated from German as "the sport of the people," refers to a movement that stresses physical activity and good health through outdoor sport. Walking events and tours make up a big part of the organization's activities.

Interesting Reading
for Walkers

The books I list below are all currently in print. There are endless others to be found in libraries and used book shops. Walkers seem to be prone to writing about walking, and there are marvelous accounts to be found of walks from the 19th century to the present.

A Walk Through Wales by Anthony Bailey. An account of a journey on foot the length of Wales, south to north, on country lanes, mountain paths, through cities, towns, and villages.

Stranger in the Forest by Eric Hansen. The story of a 1,500-mile (2,400-km) walk across Borneo—a walk of enormous physical adventure as well as an inner journey.

Walking the Trail: One Man's Journey Along the Cherokee Trail of Tears by Jerry Ellis. A 900-mile (1,440-km) walk across eight states to Oklahoma, tracing the journey of his ancestors.

The Complete Walker III by Colin Fletcher. This has been for years, and still is, the Bible for anyone who decides to walk for more than a day at a time. Everything you ever need to know about hiking/backpacking equipment is included here.

Walking Medicine: The Lifetime Guide to Preventive and Therapeutic Exercise Walking Programs by Gary Yanker and Kathy Burton, with a team of 50 medical experts. A sort of encyclopedia that looks at all the medical aspects of walking and provides a list, by state, of doctors who walk.

Stretching by Bob Anderson is considered the authoritative book on stretching.

Racewalking for Fitness by John Gray.

Walking for Sport, Health, and Fitness by Bob Carlson contains a state-by-state directory of racewalking clubs.

Fitness Walking by Therese Iknoian is part of the Human Kinetics Fitness Spectrum series.

Walking by Henry David Thoreau.

INDEX

ABOUT THE AUTHOR

© Bruce Selyem

An award-winning professional writer and an avid outdoor enthusiast, Ruth Rudner is the author of seven previous books, including four about mountain hiking. Ruth also has written numerous articles for such publications as the *Wall Street Journal*, the *New York Times*, *Walking Magazine*, *Cosmopolitan*, *Family Circle*, and many others. She has worked as an associate editor and contributing editor for *Skiing* magazine and as a contributing editor for *Self* magazine.

A member of the Outdoor Writers Association of America, Ruth has been a guest lecturer at many universities. She has been awarded a Writers Community Residency Grant to conduct master-level workshops for emerging writers in Billings, Montana. She also has been chosen by The Montana Arts Council to participate in the Tumbleweeds Literature Project for underserved communities.

Ruth attended Antioch College in Yellow Springs, Ohio; the University of Vienna Summer School in Strobl, Austria; and the Alliance Française in Paris, France. She makes her home in Bozeman, Montana, and enjoys walking and hiking in the mountains, horseback riding, and writing about her outdoor experiences.

More great books in the Outdoor Pursuit Series

Eric Seaborg and Ellen Dudley
1994 • Paper • 152 pp
Item PSEA0506 • ISBN 0-87322-506-6
$12.95 ($17.95 Canadian)

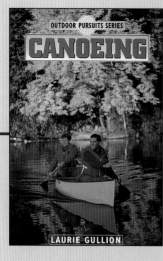

Laurie Gullion
1994 • Paper • 152 pp
Item PGUL0443 • ISBN 0-87322-443-4
$12.95 ($15.95 Canadian)

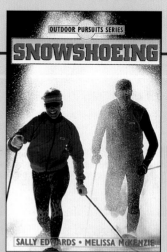

**Sally Edwards and
Melissa McKenzie**
1995 • Paper • Approx 112 pp
Item PEDW0767 • ISBN 0-87322-767-0
$13.95 ($19.50 Canadian)

Other titles in the series:
- Kayaking
- Mountain Biking
- Snowboarding
- Windsurfing
- Rock Climbing*

*Call for availability date

2335

Other books from Human Kinetics

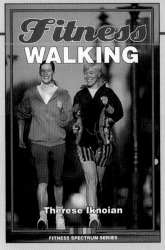

Therese Iknoian

1995 • Paper • 168 pp
Item PIKN0553 • ISBN 0-87322-553-8
$14.95 ($20.95 Canadian)

Rebecca Johnson and Bill Tulin

Foreword by James M. Rippe, MD

1995 • Paper • 216 pp
Item PJOH0655 • ISBN 0-87322-655-0
$14.95 ($19.95 Canadian)

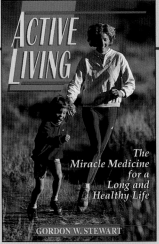

Gordon Stewart

1995 • Paper • Approx 144 pp
Item PSTE0678 • ISBN 0-87322-678-X
$13.95 ($19.50 Canadian)

To place an order: U.S. customers call
TOLL FREE 1 800 747-4457;
customers outside of U.S. use the
appropriate telephone number/address
shown in the front of this book.

Prices are subject to change.

Human Kinetics